TRUE GREAT MYSTERIES

ARNOLD P. RUBIN

SCHOLASTIC INC.
New York Toronto London Auckland Sydney

This book is dedicated
to my parents
David and Lillian Rubin

ISBN 0-590-31338-X

Published by Scholastic Inc.

12 11 10 9 8 7 6 2 3 4/9

Printed in the U.S.A. 01

Acknowledgments

I would like to offer my deepest appreciation and thanks to the many persons and organizations, who generously shared their time and wisdom with me, or otherwise were of great help, such as the staff of the National Archives, in Washington, DC.

I would, however, be especially remiss, if I did not acknowledge the following:

Mr. Jack S. Courtney, Deputy Director of Information for Scotland Yard; Commander Ernest Millen (ret.); Dr. David Kahn; Dr. Anthony R. Crawford, archivist of the George C. Marshall Research Foundation, Lexington, Virginia; Drs. Joseph E. McDade and David Fraser, of the U.S. Center for Disease Control, Atlanta, Georgia; Mr. Donald C. Drake, medical writer for *The Philadelphia Inquirer*; Mr. Roger Rosenblatt, of *The Washington Post*; Ms. Mel Fisher (Dolores); Dr. Eugene Lyon; Ms. Marian Steffens and Ms. Isabel Bodily for their research and secretarial efforts, respectively.

Last, and most definitely not least, I would like to express my gratitude to my Scholastic editor, Ms. Ann Reit, for her enthusiastic support of this project, as well as for her constructive criticism.

Introduction

The word "detective" usually brings to mind the image of a Sherlock Holmes character, in a deerstalker hat, large-bowled S-curved pipe clenched between his teeth, and over-sized magnifying glass clutched in his hand.

Currently, the portrait of a detective is more likely to be that of an individual in a dirty, loose-fitting raincoat, with a cigarette dangling from his lips, beneath a wide-brimmed, creased hat. Sometimes the cigarette is replaced with a well-chomped cigar, or even a lollypop.

Nor are these stereotypes — for that is what they are — limited to men. Today's "gumshoe" is just as likely to be a beautiful woman with long legs, golden hair spilling over her shoulders, a creamy-smooth complexion, and a gleaming-white, tooth-filled smile.

All these characters, however, belong to the realm of fiction. They are creations spawned from a writer's pen. And for many years we have been entertained, held spellbound by tales of mystery and intrigue.

But detective work is not limited to capturing crooks and solving crimes. Nor are detectives restricted to police, private eyes, or even secret agents. Instead of a trenchcoat, a detective in real life may be wearing a laboratory coat, and looking through a microscope instead of a magnifying glass. And the object of his or her pursuit may not be a criminal at all, but an organism too tiny to be seen by the eye alone.

Or the detective may be armed with nothing more lethal than a pocket-sized tape recorder, rather than a gun. And instead of prowling darkened streets may spend hours, if not days, in the well-lit corridors of libraries, "casing" book shelves, and poring over musty collections of age-yellowed documents.

Of course, there are still the crime-busting detectives around. But even they are likely to use techniques of detection not much different from their non-police counterparts. In this book, we'll meet all types of detectives, as well as villains. And each sleuth is after the same thing: cracking the case.

the literal "king's ransom." In short, "The Atocha" was buried treasure that would satisfy any soldier of fortune, and delight any historian.

Fisher had become interested in sunken treasure back in the late 1950s, at which point he had gone on treasure hunts in the Caribbean and in Central America. This was a far cry from the earlier years he had spent working on his father's chicken ranch in California.

"Mel had always been interested in pirates," recalled his wife, Dolores (or "Deo"), "and he thought that old shipwrecks would make good backgrounds for his underwater movies."

Mel and Deo had met while the elder Fisher was selling his ranch. Her parents had made an offer to purchase the chicken business. At that time, Mel Fisher had had a thriving scuba-diving supply shop located on the ranch itself.

With the sale of the ranch, Mel Fisher branched out. He went into the lobster business, selling the shell fish to restaurants. Building on this success, he opened a more elaborate diving shop — one that offered lessons, as well as equipment. And, to gain publicity for the ship, he went on television with a weekly program devoted to the world beneath the sea. The program continued for nearly five years, and Fisher got good mileage from his underwater movies.

In fact, never one to waste a good opportunity, Mel spent his and Dolores' honeymoon scuba diving and shooting movies off the Florida Keys.

Somewhat later, Mel Fisher focused his attention on searching for buried treasure. At first, the area of the searches was confined to California coastal waters. No great finds turned up, however. Certainly, no vast treasure was found. After a few years of this, Fisher tried his hand at treasure hunting in the Caribbean. It was at this point in his life that he found his first galleon, salvaging its anchor. No treasure. But the excitement at the discovery was enough to whet Fisher's appetite for more.

Unfortunately, treasure hunting is an expensive business. And although Fisher found further galleons in the waters off Panama, his search for treasure was thwarted for lack of money.

In late 1962, Mel Fisher met a man from Florida who happened to be in California at that time. The man was a member of a group of treasure hunters who had found remnants of a Spanish galleon that had sunk in 1715, near Vero Beach, Florida. They had also found some treasure, some silver.

This was enough for Fisher. Excited, Fisher put together his own team of divers, sold his worldly possessions, and moved to Florida. Fisher called his group, "Treasure Salvors, Inc." The deal was this: the men would be paid in shares of stock in the company. After one year of treasure hunting, they would be rich (Fisher hoped) . . . or they would give up.

The year began.

It was a difficult year. Money was scarce and the work was hard. Month after month, Fisher and his divers searched for treasure. They found none. Harsh seas tossed the men about as if they were puppets. Visibility was poor, limited by the tossing, turning ocean floor. Still, they continued.

The divers were on the verge of giving up when they were helped by a Mel Fisher invention. It was called the "mailbox." This apparatus, quite simply, was a kind of chute through which could be channeled the backwash of a diving ship's propellers. The effect was similar to that of a vacuum cleaner thrust into reverse gear. The "mailbox" blew away tons of sand from the seabed, exposing what lay beneath.

One day, in the spring of 1964, Fisher and his crew were investigating a galleon wreck. The mailbox was put into operation and true to form the device did its job, blowing away sand. What lay beneath the sand was what treasure hunters have prayed for for centuries.

Gold!

Hundreds of gold coins were found, and soon the hundreds became thousands. And, later, other pieces of gold would be found, and sold for considerable prices. One coin was bought for nearly $4,000. Another piece of gold went for nearly $18,000. Based on these figures, Fisher estimated that he had found treasure worth more than a million and a half dollars!

But Mel Fisher was not a man to rest on his

laurels. Past achievements were fine insofar as they meant reached goals, but accumulated wealth, with subsequent creature comforts meant little unless they could finance further, bigger, better — and richer, more exciting — expeditions.

By 1964, Mel Fisher had established his reputation as the "Treasure King of Vero Beach." It was along about this time that Fisher met another treasure hunter. This man was different from those Fisher had known before. This man was an historian, and he was interested primarily in the treasure of ancient objects.

It was through the historian that Mel Fisher first found out about "the Atocha." In the beginning, the ship held no great fascination for him. But then he found out that other treasure hunters were also interested in salvaging this prized vessel. Fisher's curiosity perked up. He decided his next quest — and conquest — would be "the Atocha."

By speaking with other divers, and consulting such books as the *Treasure Diver's Guide*, Fisher was led to believe that "the Atocha" had hit a reef and sunk in about 10 fathoms (60 feet) of water. The area he would search for was off the coast of Florida, known as "Alligator Reef." It was located in the region identified as "the Florida Keys," a 200-mile-long chain of islands.

Aside from this information, Fisher didn't

have much more to guide him. But he did have his "mailbox" to help him remove gold-hiding sand. And he had a magnetometer, a device that helped locate hidden iron.

Fisher also had the funds necessary to begin such an undertaking, which most other divers did not have. And he was in possession of leases he had purchased from the state of Florida, which again was something other divers — most of them, that is — did not benefit from. Fisher was given permission to explore 18,000 square miles of territory that made up the seabed. He paid for this authorization, and he would have to pay the state of Florida additional sums if he found any treasure that he wanted to recover.

It was not long before Fisher found a galleon; it was not "the Atocha." The search continued. Other shipwrecks were found; none was "the Atocha." With each wreck, Fisher put a buoy to mark the site. In return for a fee, he reached agreements with other treasure hunters, giving them permission to recover any wealth that lay beneath the sea in these long-lost vessels. Each salvager was given a percentage of the haul. In any event, it soon became clear that Fisher's hunt for "the Atocha" wasn't going anywhere. Months dragged into years, but no "Atocha."

Fisher needed more help, more information. He flew to Spain and hired researchers to pore over centuries-old documents that might yield clues to the exact site of "the Atocha's" underwater grave. One researcher would work at the Archives of Madrid; another would send him information from the Archive of the Indies, in Seville.

But the researchers kept telling him the same thing: look in the Matecumbe Keys. This, however, was the area in the Florida Straits where Fisher and his crew had been hunting all along for "the Atocha." And where, time and again, they had come up empty-handed. Nor was he alone. Others who had hunted for the ship and plumbed the depths of these waters had sought "the Atocha" in vain. Obviously, they, and Fisher, were doing something wrong.

But what?

The years went by. Fisher and his crew had optimistically — some might say, recklessly — predicted that they would find "the Atocha" in a matter of weeks. But now the search had been going on for years and they seemed no closer to their treasure ship and the fortune it was reported to contain.

Meanwhile, Fisher continued to find galleons. One in particular, in fact, proved to be quite valuable, both in terms of history and in terms of material riches. But any money Fisher earned from that wreck had to be balanced against the costs he had thus far incurred in his searching and salvaging operations. Beyond this, Fisher had lost precious time that he might have been using to look for "the Atocha."

And all the while, Fisher had to be concerned with raising money to keep his search going. Some of the money he got came from the sale of artifacts he had recovered from other wrecks. Other funds resulted from selling stock and shares of treasure. In short, Mel Fisher was offering people — for a price — part of his dream, a dream that he felt was going to be the reality of a recovered "Atocha."

Day after day, Fisher drove his crew — and himself — in the hunt for their elusive prey. To some people, Mel Fisher was a man obsessed. And his obsession was a Spanish galleon that had not sailed the earth's waters for hundreds of years. "The Atocha" was something that Mel Fisher lived and breathed. From the waters off Miami to the waters off Key West, the Fisher expedition relentlessly chased "the Atocha." In foul weather, as well as in fair, Fisher continued his stubborn odyssey.

Would he ever give up? The 1960s had come and gone without Mel Fisher finding a single artifact, a single coin, anything that might indicate to him and to others that he had found the final resting place of "the Atocha." It was as if the ship and its long-dead crew taunted the treasure hunter, as if it had a life and mobility of its own, forever eluding the sight and touch of a man who had spent so much time in pursuit.

Mel Fisher returned to Spain.

In February of 1970, Mel and Deo Fisher arrived in Seville, Spain, in search of an old friend from their Vero Beach days. His name was Eugene Lyon. Gene Lyon was a different treasure hunter from Mel Fisher. The treasures the former man sought lay in the richness of history, in seeking knowledge for its own sake, knowledge of times and peoples long, long ago. The latter man, by contrast, was an adventurer who would — and did — risk life and limb in search of material things. Mel Fisher did this both for the wealth those things offered, as well as for the excitement of the hunt — and discovery — itself.

This is not to suggest that Gene Lyon was not interested in treasure. It just means that it was less of an obsession than it was with Mel Fisher.

These were the two men who now faced each other at the Archives of the Indies in Seville. At one time, Seville had been the center of Colonial Spain's trade with the New World. And the Archive of the Indies contained a vast storehouse of invaluable documents pertaining to that trade.

Fisher had known that Lyon would be here, researching his doctoral thesis in the history of Latin America. The treasure hunter had hoped that Lyon, who was fluent in Spanish, would be able to help him pinpoint the location of "the Atocha."

Indeed, before coming to Spain, Fisher had written Gene Lyon requesting his help. And if any man could help him, Fisher thought, it would be this scholar who was so familiar with Spanish history and language. As a result of Fisher's letter, Lyon began to do some research on "the Atocha." He was looking for information pertaining to the ship in 1622, the year it sank. He thought that Spanish tax records of that time would record the sinking of the galleon.

Lyon was right.

In one set of documents, he found a list of the cargo "the Atocha" had carried. He sent the information to Fisher, who was now in Spain.

It didn't take Fisher long to get to the point. Before he had left Lyon in Spain, Fisher had promised the scholar a reward of $10,000 if he could direct the treasure hunter within a quarter mile of where "the Atocha" now rested.

Truly, this was a large sum of money. But it was nothing compared to the amount of work that lay ahead of Lyon if he was going to help Fisher. And he was.

In the Archive of the Indies, there are literally *millions* of documents related to Colonial Spain and its trade with the New World, following the voyages of Columbus. Some documents are indexed. Others are not.

Just as Mel Fisher was not the first man to

hunt "the Atocha," neither was Gene Lyon the first man to research data on the ship. So the treasure hunters knew of earlier efforts to salvage the vessel. None of this was of any great help to Fisher and crew. All he did know was what he did not know. That is, he did not know where the ship was. He didn't even know if the ship had been found centuries before, and its cargo recovered. Perhaps he had been looking for a ghost ship after all.

And so, Gene Lyon, like Mel Fisher, was conducting a search based on two vital pieces of information: the name of the ship ("Atocha") and the year it sank (1622). This much was common knowledge. This and the fact — if it was a fact (as reported by earlier researchers) — that the treasure ship had been sunk in the Matecumbe Keys, off the Florida coast. But it had been this area that Fisher had spent so many years exploring so unsuccessfully. It was a big ocean out there in the Atlantic, and unless Fisher had more information — from Lyon he hoped — he could spend the rest of his life in endless forays up, down, and around offshore Florida. Time, money, and energy had their limits. If Fisher was going to continue his quest, Lyon was going to have to provide the key that would unlock the mystery.

But where should Lyon begin looking for that key?

In his search for documents, Gene Lyon was

aided by his scholarship, knowledge, experience, determination, reasoning — and not a little bit of luck. Thumbing through papers regarding trade, Lyon found information concerning the Spanish fleet in 1622.

Paydirt!

The documents referred to "the Atocha" and the rest of the fleet of which it had been a part. Gradually, Lyon was able to reconstruct events that had taken place nearly 350 years before.

The essential information was this: "The Atocha" was part of a fleet of warships that was charged with protecting Spain's commercial vessels. But the galleon also carried valuable goods as it made its long voyage back to Spain from the New World.

So, in addition to 20 bronze cannon, the 600-ton "Atocha" transported 901 silver bars, 161 disks or bars made of gold, and more than one quarter million coins made of silver. The total value of the galleon's cargo today would be worth millions of dollars.

On September 4, 1622, "the Atocha" left Havana, Cuba' harbor and headed for Spain. On this return voyage it would enter the Straits of Florida, not too far from the Florida Keys.

It would also run smack into the teeth of a hurricane. The storm drove "the Atocha" and her sister ships closer to the keys and their deadly reefs. On September 6, "the Atocha" ran aground and was trapped. The terrifying winds began to chew the ship to pieces.

The final toll taken by the hurricane was staggering. Hundreds of lives were lost among those who had been on "the Atocha" and other ships in the fleet. In monetary terms, the loss of the cargo on these ships was estimated as being as high as 250 million dollars.

Spain found out its great loss from survivors' reports. Attempts were made to salvage "the Atocha," but by that time another hurricane had swept the area and had further torn apart the remains of the galleon. Still, some efforts continued, although it seems that by the end of the century Spain had pretty much lost hope of ever recovering "the Atocha."

But if Spain had given up, Mel Fisher had not. Meanwhile, Gene Lyon was studying thousands of pages of Spanish documents, many years old. In one pile of papers, Lyon found the key Fisher had been hoping the scholar would find. Lyon recalled that exciting moment:

"I was looking through an index for some material relating to Spanish Florida and ran across an audit of the accounts of the salvage of a ship on the coast of Florida. I felt immediately it was from the 1622 ships. . . . And, on this last page, it used the words that I saw for the first time — 'Cayos del Marquez.' "

What exactly had Lyon found among those worm-eaten documents?

The phrase, "Cayos del Marquez," meant "Keys of the Marquis." But Lyon's find meant more than just another name in a document. It was a specific place that he had just identified. And by studying maps of the Florida Keys, going back to the 16th-century, Lyon realized what Mel Fisher had been doing wrong all along.

Fisher, as was common with other "Atocha" hunters, had been searching for the galleon in the Matecumbe Keys. But Lyon now had discovered that the Spanish used "Matecumbe" to refer to the entire chain of islands that made up the Florida Keys, with the exception of the distant Dry Tortugas.

What did all this mean?

It meant, quite simply, that Mel Fisher had spent years and a small fortune looking for "the Atocha" in the wrong place! In fact, Fisher had been searching for the prized ship 100 miles away from where he should have been searching!

Lyon quickly sent this vital news to Fisher.

In a sense, researchers of historical events were now directing Fisher's hunt for "the Atocha." First, Lyon had directed Fisher to a site 100 miles away from where the treasure hunter had originally been searching. Then, another researcher told Fisher he should be looking east of the Marquesas. Later, Lyon discovered that the researcher had erred. Fisher, Lyon said, should be hunting for "the Atocha" *west* of the Marquesas!

Once more Mel Fisher began his relentless pursuit of "the Atocha." Night and day, the Fisher expedition hunted for this Spanish galleon that had been resting beneath the sea through four centuries.

And still it remained hidden from Mel Fisher.

The treasure hunter seemed to find everything but the ship in the waters of the Florida Straits. Fisher found old airplane wrecks, oil drums, unexploded torpedoes, and more modern ship wrecks.

But no "Atocha."

Another year came and went without "the Atocha" being found. Costs were mounting. Fisher was spending as much as a thousand dollars each day of the search. At one point the search almost cost more than money — it almost cost Fisher his life. While investigating what he thought was a cannon, Fisher nearly struck a mine that had survived World War II. Had Fisher hit that mine or one of the hundreds of others in that particular area, doubtless he would have been killed. For a mine that could sink a ship could easily rip a man into pieces.

Still, Mel Fisher would not give up. He had already invested too much of his life in this venture. Even though he was spending money as fast as he earned it, and even though so many years seemed to push "the Atocha" farther and farther away, Mel Fisher would not quit. It would not take much encouragement to keep him going in his quest for the ghostly galleon.

One day Fisher received that encouragement. He was led to believe that he had finally found "the Atocha." Fisher had been diving when he came upon a musket ball. Then a huge anchor was found, an anchor three times the size of an average man.

And then came the gold.

One of Fisher's divers discovered a chain that was half as long as the anchor, or eight feet in length. The chain turned out to be made of gold. But despite Fisher's joy at this find, he had no proof that this chain had come from "the Atocha." Months later, he found himself still searching.

Fisher had found the anchor in June of 1971, which was the first year that he could point to something concrete that may have been connected to "the Atocha."

One year later, Fisher still had found nothing that would conclusively prove he had found the treasure ship. By late 1972, it seemed that Mel Fisher had failed at long last. All the years of searching, all the false leads, all the near misses, all the bloated claims, and the eternal — but unrewarded optimism — had led to naught. If only Fisher had found some item that could definitely be linked to "the Atocha," at least he would have done what so many others had failed to do for centuries. But at this point that did not seem likely.

To make matters worse, Fisher had just about run out of money. And the weather had turned bad. Furthermore, people who had lent Fisher money had now grown tired of waiting for a return on their investment in his dream.

And still Fisher would not call it quits.

He embarked on a successful fund-raising campaign. His funds included $20,000 from the highly-respected National Geographic Society. The organization, which publishes *National Geographic* magazine, was hopeful that it could produce a television documentary based on Fisher's discovery of "the Atocha."

The society had become a part of Mel Fisher's dream, which in turn had evolved into a huge gamble. But the new infusion of funds gave further impetus to Fisher's search . . . the funds, plus the nearly fanatical loyalty of his crew and close circle of supporters.

In the fall of 1972, Fisher had managed to find some coins minted before 1622. But there was no way of telling whether or not these had come from "the Atocha." It seemed as if Fisher had reached a dead end. He had been hunting "the Atocha" for many years now — three in the Marquesas alone.

Where was that ship?

Perhaps Eugene Lyon, the scholar now working in Spain, might be able to come up with the answer. Then again, perhaps not. Finding documents in the Archive of the Indies, in Seville, was like looking for treasure itself. Only the sands covering the treasure Lyon was seeking were the sands of time. And what was he looking for, anyway?

Years earlier, Lyon had found a summary of the records of the cargo "the Atocha" had carried. This he had sent to Fisher. Now, however, Lyon had located a more detailed cargo list and had it transferred to microfilm. He had good reason for this action; the list was 2,000 pages long!

Lyon pressed on. He was looking for a map that might indicate where "the Atocha" had gone down. He found none. But the information Lyon was able to glean from the stacks of centuries-old documents was at least confirmation that Mel Fisher was looking in the correct general area.

If Lyon could not be more specific about where the Spanish galleon now lay, at least he could help Fisher identify "the Atocha" when, and if, the treasure seeker finally found it. For example, in translating the cargo manifest, Lyon realized that the hundreds of bars of silver "the Atocha" had carried were listed by weight. So each could be recognized as having come from that ship. In the absence of any further data from Lyon regarding the location of "the Atocha," the ship's manifest seemed to be Fisher's only hope that he could prove the identity of the ship.

Gene Lyon returned to Florida.

Spring, 1973. So many years had gone by in the search for "the Atocha" that some persons connected with it couldn't even remember when the adventure had begun. The years seemed to blur, to meld into each other. And the hunt for "the Atocha" had been marked by high and low points; 1971 had been high, 1972 had been low. What would 1973 be?

The year seemed to start out on a hopeful note. Fisher's financial troubles apparently were behind him, at least for the time being. He was also able to expand his fleet of search ships. Perhaps for once Fisher's motto, "Today's the day," would indeed come true, and he would find "the Atocha," after so much agonizing disappointment.

One day in May, aided by clear weather, the divers descended as they had done countless times over the long years. There was little to distinguish this day from the hundreds of others that had passed. Suddenly, the divers discovered what appeared to be a treasure trove: coins made of silver, cannonballs made of stone, some made of iron, swords, and muskets. The more the divers searched, the more they found. As the month of May drew to a close, the coins numbered in the hundreds. Soon the hundreds turned to thousands. The divers nicknamed the area, in which the coins had been found, "the Bank of Spain."

By now Gene Lyon was in Florida. On shore, he studied the latest find by Fisher's divers. Although much work remained to be done in cleaning centuries of crust from the coins, there seemed little doubt that Fisher had found Spanish coins. Further, the silver coins were identified as having come from Peru and Mexico — and therefore were similar to those "the Atocha" carried when it went down in 1622. One coin in particular thrilled Lyon; it had been minted in what is known now as Colombia. Yet, before this coin had been found, historians had no idea that such coins had been struck at that time, and in that place. It was almost as if Fisher had found "the Atocha" itself.

Now it seemed as if Fisher could do no wrong. One magnificent discovery followed another.

The following month, Fisher's son, Dirk, came up with an astrolobe. It was an invaluable find. The astrolobe — a device used to help navigate ships — is thought to be over 400 years old! In all likelihood, this astrolobe was similar to one that might have been on "the Atocha." There was no way of knowing for sure. But this was of little consequence because of its great value to historians, and because it seemed to justify Mel Fisher's unbounded optimism and determination.

It was Father's Day, and son Kim presented Mel Fisher with a present: two big gold pieces. Father and son estimated the pieces to weigh about 10 pounds each. There no longer was any doubt that Mel Fisher had found a wreck containing treasure. There was still no way, at this point, of determining whether or not Fisher had found "the Atocha." He seemed so terribly close, and yet so terribly far, from his prize.

July 4th — Independence Day. Fisher and his crew were still mining the depths, making "withdrawals" from "the Bank of Spain." A gold and coral rosary was found. And then another Fisher son, Kane, found what seemed to him to be a loaf of bread. Instead, he found he had discovered a single silver ingot. Then other bars of silver were found. And ballast stones. These stones were used on ships like "the Atocha" to provide stability.

Could it be that Mel Fisher had finally found "the Atocha"?

Gene Lyon was determined to find out.

Each silver bar carried a serial number. Lyon now had the exhausting task of comparing the serial numbers on the silver bars with those listed on the manifest he had microfilmed, which listed the cargo of "the Atocha." The weights of the bars would also have to be confirmed in similar fashion.

There was no doubt in Fisher's mind that he

had found "the Atocha." This despite the fact that Lyon warned that the Spanish might have repeated serial numbers because they had produced so many.

But Mel Fisher had come too far over too long a period of time to have his spirits dampened, or optimism and faith eroded, by the possibility of such a coincidence. In Fisher's mind, the serial numbers and weights on the silver bars would match those listed on the manifest of "the Atocha."

He was right.

Now came the final test to prove the bars had come from "the Atocha." Their weights should be identical to those on the ship's manifest.

Mel Fisher called a press conference. His victory — or defeat — was going to be played out before the media, which included television.

On the manifest of "the Atocha" was listed silver bar 4584, which carried a weight of 63.6 pounds. A freight scale had been preset at 63.6 pounds. If that was the weight of the bar 4584 Mel Fisher had found, then the needle should not stray from the preset weight of 63.6 pounds.

The bar was placed on the scale.

It weighed in at exactly 63.6 pounds!

Fisher had his match!

"We have found 'the Atocha,'" Mel Fisher announced to all who had assembled for the weigh-in ceremony.

The other bars also were matched.

And so 1973 appeared to be the year Mel Fisher had found "the Atocha," the ship that had consumed him for so many years. By the time the year was out, Fisher had recovered treasure from the wreckage of "the Atocha" in excess of $1 million.

But the story of his search was far from over, and the full price for the recovered bounty had not yet been paid.

The summer of his incredible discovery saw the death of an 11-year-old boy who had been visiting one of Fisher's ships. While in the water, the youngster had accidentally been caught in the vessel's propellers.

Fisher's problems began to mount following that tragedy. He began to have problems with the law. The U.S. government was investigating a complaint about the way Fisher kept records of his financial dealings. His expenses mounted. On top of all these setbacks, which were part of the price Fisher was now paying for having hunted and found spoils from "the Atocha," the state of Florida wanted its share of the treasure — 25 percent.

Thus, 1973 was a year of incredible highs for Fisher, as well as incredible lows.

By the following year, 1974, Fisher's situation was somewhat improved. The U.S. government ended its investigation of the way Fisher did business; in return, Fisher agreed to follow the relevant laws. With the cloud of prosecution lifted, Fisher was again able to raise money to continue his search for the remainder of "the Atocha's" treasure.

Not everyone, however, was convinced that Fisher had indeed found "the Atocha." Mel Fisher was "hot," a controversial figure. Even Florida officials — who held Fisher's treasure before taking their one-quarter cut would not support the fact that Fisher had found "the Atocha." And it would be difficult for Fisher to raise additional funds without getting his hands on the treasure.

March, 1975. The state of Florida was ready to divide the treasure between itself and Mel Fisher. But the question of ownership was one that dragged on for years. It was not that government officials denied Fisher had found treasure. Rather, it was a question of how much of a share the state of Florida should get. And how much of a share the government of the United States should get. This issue of jurisdiction is one that has lasted to the time this is being written (February, 1979). This continues to be part of the price Mel Fisher has paid in his search for "the Atocha."

To sum up this question of jurisdiction: in 1978, the U.S. dropped its claim to the treasure. And the U.S. Supreme Court ruled "the Atocha" had been claimed in waters beyond Florida's jurisdiction. Florida then argued that it had a valid contract with Fisher for 25 percent of the treasure he recovered. A federal judge disagreed, and the issue continued to be fought over in the courts.

Did Mel Fisher really find "the Atocha"?

To answer that question, let's go back to 1975.

Gene Lyon, Mel Fisher's friend and scholar, had returned to Spain. He was prepared to do more research. Lyon was interested in finding out more about the cargo "the Atocha" had been carrying when it sank in 1622. He was especially interested in the bronze cannon "the Atocha" had on board. Lyon found documents listing the serial numbers on the cannons attached to "the Atocha." Mel Fisher had found no such cannons at this point, but Lyon copied the numbers . . . just in case. After concluding his research, Lyon decided to head back to Florida.

Meanwhile, Mel Fisher had finally divided his treasure with Florida, although the dispute about the 25 percent remained. In any event, Mel Fisher had, by this time, been hunting "the Atocha" treasure in the waters of the Marquesas for six years.

There was no doubt in his mind that the treasure he had found had been from "the Atocha." Still, he wanted more proof, proof that once and for all time would silence attacks on his reputation as a treasure hunter, and as an honest man.

July 13, 1975. An archeologist hired by Mel

Fisher believed that the rest of "the Atocha's" treasure lay in deeper water than Fisher had been exploring for the past half decade. Fisher's first-born son, Dirk, decided to test this theory. He dove where the water deepened. For a while he disappeared beneath the waves. And then he returned, screaming, shouting, swirling his arms above the surface.

Dirk Fisher had found cannons, and they were made of bronze!

Young Fisher had found five such cannons, in fact. The archeologist seemed to have been right. Each weighed more than a ton.

More cannons were found, a total of nine — all made of bronze. Not all could be identified; their physical condition was too poor. But four could be. As with the silver bars found two years earlier, in 1973, the numbers and weights of the cannon were compared with those Gene Lyon had brought back from Spain.

They matched!

There no longer was any doubt.

After years of searching, Mel Fisher had finally found the object of his obsession — "the Atocha," "the Big A."

True, the ship was not found intact. Nor did Fisher find the main store of riches. But he had done what no other person had done before. Mel Fisher had identified the remains of a vessel that had neither been seen nor touched by another human being for more than 300 years.

But he paid a terrible price for his historic finds.

On July 19, 1975, less than a week after the dramatic discovery of the bronze cannons by Dirk Fisher, tragedy struck. One of the vessels that made up Mel Fisher's search fleet sank. Several persons drowned. Among them were 21-year-old Dirk Fisher, and his wife, Angel.

By 1979, Mel Fisher had spent about 12 of his 57 years searching for the remains of a Spanish galleon that sank in a storm off the coast of Florida more than 350 years ago.

In the interim, millions of dollars had been made, and spent. Ships had been sunk. Lives had been lost. And a vast treasure had been restored to the world, some *15,000* pieces.

Still, success had not written the end to Mel Fisher's search for the "motherlode" of "the Atocha."

"This (1979) is the year," said Dolores Fisher, speaking by phone from Treasure Salvors, Inc., in Key West, Florida.

Or, perhaps, the next?

Chapter 2

THE GREAT TRAIN ROBBERY

Through the darkness of the British countryside at night, brightened by a late summer moon, the diesel-powered train roared down the tracks. This was no ordinary train. Against the side of the green engine was a gold symbol representing the Crown of England. The train was the Royal Mail Carrier for the British government, en route from Glasgow, Scotland, to London, England. And the cargo it transported was worth the equivalent of $7 million in British currency.

At the throttle was a veteran engineer. As he watched the British landscape disappear past the locomotive's 75-miles-per-hour speed, he had no reason to be worried. In the 125 years of these "traveling post offices," not one had been robbed.

August 8, 1963. The train was only about 45 minutes away from its destination, Euston Station in London. Its present location was the agricultural district of Leighton Buzzard. The time was about 3 a.m.

As the postal train approached Cheddington, which was less than 40 miles from London, the engineer noticed that the track signals were against him. There was amber, the first signal to contend with, which acted as a precautionary traffic light, and which caused the engineer to slow the train. Finally, a red light, a little farther on, made the engineer stop the train completely.

An assistant to the engineer left the train in search of a phone box along the tracks from which he could call ahead. The engineer had expressed concern because of an oddity he had noticed in the signals. Although the signal halting the train was red, the one that followed it was green.

The assistant disappeared into the darkness, walking along the outline of the tracks. When he reached the telephone he discovered that the phone's wires had been cut, rendering it useless. There was little else for him to do at that point but return to the train.

As the assistant turned and began to retrace his steps, a figure jumped out of the night and hurled himself at the trainman. Before the engineer's assistant realized what was happening, the figure crashed into him and sent him tumbling down the incline that ran parallel to the tracks.

Stunned, he sat on the bottom of the grassy embankment. As he regained his breath, he may have thought of putting up a struggle, or at least trying to warn his partner by crying out. But if he had had any such thoughts, a harsh voice quickly cut them off.

"If you shout, I'll kill you," the voice said.

The assistant didn't need to be told more than once.

"All right mate, I'm on your side," he told his assailant.

Meanwhile, aboard train number D326, the engineer awaited his fellow trainman. Not only was he unaware of the man's fate, but he also was not aware of the group of figures that gathered in the darkness outside his cab.

The attack on the train began as members of the gang entered the engine room, surrounding the engineer. He tried to fight them back, but a blow to his head by one of the bandits sent the engineer sprawling.

Quickly, the gang of hooded men gained control of the train. Both the engineer, now injured, and his assistant (who had been taken aboard by his captors), lay on the floor of the cab.

Once in charge, the robbers separated the engine and the two cars behind it from the rest of the train. These two cars carried the most valuable freight, or HVPs (for "High Value Packages").

All the while, the other train personnel calmly went about their business of sorting mail. They were not aware that they were in the middle of the richest train robbery in railroad history.

It was the intention of the robbers to move the train farther down the tracks to Bridego Bridge, about a mile away. At that point they would then make off with their loot.

Unfortunately for them, they could not make the train move. The gang had brought their own driver with them, but he suddenly developed a bad case of nerves and was unable to get the train started. Instead, the bandits forced a bleeding engineer to drive.

At the bridge, the engineer was ordered to stop the train. Beneath the bridge was a country road, and the two trainmen were ordered from the train and down the embankment. Again, they were handcuffed. They remained so while the train robbers unloaded their booty.

The booty consisted of scores of mailbags, each filled with British currency. The mailbags, after being taken from the train, were loaded on a waiting truck.

Satisfied they had taken enough, the robbers fled in a truck, leaving the engineer, his assistant and the postal clerks behind. And British banks were now poorer by some $7 million.

Britain was in an uproar over the "Great Train

Robbery," as it was quickly dubbed. Some people even went so far as to call it the "crime of the century."

An international manhunt was begun in an effort to capture gang members. And British insurers of the banks' money offered rewards adding up to nearly three quarters of a million dollars. They were joined by one bank, which was uninsured, and the Post Office.

As a result, British police were overwhelmed with phone calls from people claiming to have information about the robbery, and hoping to share the reward money.

One of those who called was a man who tended cows. Another was a widow. Unlike most calls following the robbery, theirs would be of help to police, who were frustrated by lack of solid clues. This was despite an army of law enforcement officials who swept over the scene of the robbery.

Still, they tried to make the little that they did know work to their advantage. The police knew, for example, that the robbers had warned the train crew not to move for half an hour. The police therefore told reporters that the robbers had to have been within 30 miles of the robbery site, because the thieves could not have gone farther in that period of time. Actually, the police didn't know this to be true for sure. Perhaps, however, the gang members might panic and, in attempting to flee, might run straight into British police who had been combing the countryside.

The herdsman heard the police report and recalled the house of a farmer about a mile away. He thought that there was something odd about that house and decided to investigate it by himself. Although he didn't know who they were, the herdsman knew that the property — Leatherslade Farm — had undergone a change in owners.

His suspicions were further strengthened when he reached Leatherslade Farm and saw no signs of life. All he saw were some vehicles, one of which was wrapped in canvas. He decided to call the police. And so he did, but there was no immediate response from them. He phoned again and tried to convince police officials that he was no prankster.

Meanwhile, the widow also tried to tip off police as she recalled seeing what she had originally thought were British troops training near the robbery site.

Police were to find both calls helpful. These were alert citizens responding to police information, or at least to police theories. Events that would seem ordinary to any passerby now caused local residents to look at them with a jaundiced eye. The herdsman, for example, might not have been skeptical at seeing the windows at Leatherslade Farm framing thick curtains. These curtains concealed what lay inside. Those in the farmhouse, however, could see out because a slight space had been made for them to do so. And if the herdsman now wondered what the owners had to hide, he might well also have wondered why they had an army truck on the farm, and why it was covered with yellow paint. Perhaps the answer lay in the police report that the trainman (the engineer's assistant) had seen an army truck at the time of the robbery.

Thus, it would also be logical for the widow to be suspicious of the "soldiers" she had observed. For police had requested that the British think about anything they might have considered out of the ordinary on the evening prior to the robbery — such as military transports.

The most important call, however, came from the herdsman. On August 13, less than one week after the holdup, British police entered Leatherslade Farm. They quickly realized that they had discovered the thieves' lair.

Indeed, it was a treasure chest of clues. And detectives and police scientists eagerly pored over every inch of the farm, the house, and the contents and objects that lay within and without.

Among the items the police found were the following: a "Monopoly" game; sleeping bags and blankets; a supply of food, some of which had been left over from previous meals; and military vehicles, such as the kind the engineer's assistant had reported seeing.

Police also recovered some of the 120 mailbags

that had been stolen from the train — along with the ripped pieces of paper used to tie money into bundles. These wrappers carried the identifying marks of the banks whose money had been taken.

Furthermore, it was standard operating procedure in such cases for police experts to dust for fingerprints. Using a special kind of powder, fingerprint specialists can take an impression of the loops that line the tips of our fingers. It is said that no two fingerprints are alike. And by comparing prints found at the scene of a crime to those of a person — or at least with a person's fingerprint record — a link can be established.

In addition to fingerprints, police also check for a *modus operandi*, or *method of working*. For example, if a safe is robbed, police would check to see how it was done. Was an explosive such as dynamite used? Or was a corrosive chemical, such as acid, used to burn through the safe? Police would then ask themselves what robbers they have captured in the past have been known to specialize in breaking into safes, either with the use of acid or dynamite.

With the train robbers, police asked themselves what large-scale robberies had been committed in recent years, and who was involved with them. They hoped this would lead them to the bandits.

Another source of information for the police is the tipster, or informant. Some informers provide tips to the police in exchange for money.

Others talk about what they know in exchange for favors they may need at the time, or in the future.

As far as the train robbery was concerned, British detectives were tipped off that the men whom they were looking for were members of a gang whose home base was the city of London. This helped narrow the search focus point.

The first break in the case came with the discovery of Leatherslade Farm and all that it revealed.

Would there be a second?

About the time Leatherslade Farm made national headlines, two men rented a garage outside of London. The person to whom they paid the money was the widow of a police officer. She immediately became suspicious when one of the pair took out a large sum of money from which he proceeded to pay her. The woman decided to test her suspicions. She phoned the police.

The men were arrested.

In addition, police recovered the British equivalent of about $150,000 from a car the two men had left in the woman's garage. In another vehicle in the garage, police found more than $200,000. There now was no longer any doubt in the minds of police that these vast sums had come from the great train robbery.

Police were further helped by the fact that British money, as with American currency, contains serial numbers. With part of the stolen money in their possession, police sought to track down the rest. They made public some of the serial numbers that had been recorded by personnel from banks which had lost money in the robbery.

This led them to another suspect. He had bought one of the cars from which police had recovered stolen money. His picture (he had a criminal record) had been identified by the car salesman.

By now, furthermore, the work of fingerprints experts was beginning to pay off. The fingerprints lifted from various items at Leatherslade Farm (such as the "Monopoly" board) were identified as belonging to men with whom British law enforcement officials were familiar. In fact, police were interested in talking to virtually anyone they knew who had been involved in thievery, and particularly those known to associate with the suspects police had identified thus far.

One day, about a week after the great train robbery, a man and his wife went walking through the woods. In the course of their excursion they stumbled upon some luggage. When they further examined the contents of the bags, they found money. They called the police.

When the police arrived, they confiscated the property the couple had found, along with additional sums turned up by further exploration of the surrounding area. Included in the haul was nearly $300,000 and a receipt. The receipt had been issued to still another couple who had eaten at a certain reastaurant in Germany.

More pieces to the puzzle had been found. In seeking further parts to the mystery, police asked themselves this question: Who had purchased Leatherslade Farm for the robbers?

Upon investigating, police discovered that the purchase agent was a law firm. And one of the employees in this law firm was the same man to whom the German restaurant receipt had been issued. This receipt had been found among the almost $300,000 the police had previously recovered in the woods.

In this manner, and by comparing fingerprints on recovered items to prints belonging to persons who had criminal records, the police began to expand their list of suspects.

The fingerprint analysts had done a tremendous job in matching the prints of those suspects who had worn gloves during their activities at Leatherslade. The robbers had not realized that their gloves — made wet by perspiration — had gotten smaller. Thus, the lines on the inside of their hands could more easily press through the material and mark anything they touched with their own particular identification.

British officials decided to begin the trials of those men whom the police had arrested and charged. By the time the trials began — January, 1964, less than six months after the robbery of the Glasgow-to-London mail train — British police had identified 15 suspects. (Actually, they had identified 16 prime suspects, but one was eventually found innocent.) These were: Ronald Biggs, Roy James, James Hussey, Thomas Wisbey, Robert Welch, Ronald Edwards, Gordon Goody, Bruce Field, Lennie Field, John Wheater, Roger Cordrey, Bill Boal, Bruce Reynolds, James White, and Charles Wilson.

Not all, however, were in police hands as the trials began. Three — James White, Bruce Reynolds, and Ronald Edwards — were still on the run, as fugitives.

The trials lasted through spring. Hundreds of pieces of evidence — from fingerprints on the "Monopoly" board to the recovered train money — were introduced. Expert witnesses were heard.

There were a number of charges, but the universal one was that of having conspired to steal mail from the train.

The task of the court was made somewhat easier when Roger Cordrey pleaded guilty and thus had himself removed from the proceedings.

What evidence did police have against the others?

The evidence against Bill Boal and Gordon Goody was particularly interesting. In the case of Boal, police experts found traces of yellow paint on a door knob, which had been found in a jacket that belonged to him. An analysis of the paint's properties revealed it to match those of the paint used to color vehicles linked to the robbery.

The evidence of the paint was also used against Goody. Police had taken a pair of shoes from his apartment. An examination of the paint found at the bottom of the shoes was to determine the relationship between those stains and smears on the pedals of the robbery vehicle.

They matched.

For Lennie Field, Brian Field (no relation), and John Wheater, there was a common link. That link was Leatherslade Farm, the train robbers' hideout.

Lennie Field had been named as the buyer of Leatherslade Farm in a contract negotiated by John Wheater. In addition to the legal document which Lennie Field had signed, there was correspondence between John Wheater and an attorney acting on behalf of the previous owners.

As for Brian Field, he had met the owner's wife, who had taken him on a tour of the farm, after he had expressed an interest in purchasing it. And with Field at the time, was Lennie Field.

To Ronald Biggs fell the task of explaining how his fingerprints came to be on a number of items taken from Leatherslade Farm.

Their own fingerprints also provided eloquent testimony against Thomas Wisbey, James Hussey, and Robert Welch. Their prints had been found at Leatherslade or on one of the vehicles connected with the train holdup.

It would be difficult for these men — as well as for the rest, Roy James and Charles Wilson — to deny their connection to Leatherslade, because of print identification. This, however, did not stop them from issuing such denials, nor trying to explain away the evidence against them.

It would now be up to a jury to decide who was telling the truth, and who was not. In the end, the jury would believe the innocence of only one man. For the remainder of those in custody, the jury issued another verdict.

Guilty!

Each now stood before the presiding judge to hear his sentences pronounced. The severity of those sentences — the length of time for which they would be condemned to remain in prison — would shock the nation. Even upon appeal, those sentences would be for many years.

Robert Welch, Gordon Goody, Thomas Wisbey, Roy James, Charles Wilson, Ronald Biggs, and James Hussey each was sentenced to 30 years in prison. None of these men was older than 34..

Brian Field was given five years.

William Boal received 14.

Roger Cordrey also was sentenced to 14 years in prison.

Leonard Field got five.

John Wheater was sentenced to three.

Despite the harshness of the sentences, and the fact that all the major actors in the great train robbery drama had been identified, the play was far from over.

Three men were still wanted by police.

Where were James White, Bruce Reynolds, and Ronald Edwards?

The hunt for the fugitive train robbers was an international one. When, for example, police had been seeking Roy James, they had hunted in nearly 80 countries. (James stood trial along with the others in 1964). As it turned out, James was captured — as a result of a tip — in England itself, not very far from Scotland Yard.

Furthermore, while police were searching for White, Reynolds, and Edwards, the fugitive list expanded. Train robbers Charles Wilson and Ronald Biggs escaped from prison. And a not-so-merry chase was on.

Bruce Reynolds fled England and headed for France. Eventually, he ended up in Mexico City, Mexico.

Ronald Edwards went to Belgium. He had smuggled himself out of England by boat. Aided by a phony passport, he entered Germany. While in Germany he underwent plastic surgery. He hoped that by changing his appearance police would not be able to recognize him. His fingerprints, however, remained the same.

Charles Wilson and Ronald Biggs went to France. Biggs also underwent plastic surgery.

The fugitives seemed to follow one another from country to country, with the police hot on their heels. Being a fugitive is a haunting life, no matter how much money a law evader has. The constant fear of arrest, the high life style, the feeling of rootlessness all take their toll of the human spirit.

The years went by.

In the spring of 1966, James White was arrested, in England. A British newspaper had published his picture, along with those of Ronald Biggs, Bruce Reynolds, Ronald Edwards, and Charles Wilson. White had been recognized and this was reported to British police. Faced with the evidence against him (his fingerprints had been matched to those on a trailer in which police had found $82,000), James White pleaded guilty.

He was sentenced to 18 years in prison.

It was about this time that Ronald Edwards decided to surrender. He wanted to arrange a deal with the police. White's sentence had been a long one, but it certainly was not as long as the others had received who had originally stood trial in 1964.

In September of 1966, Ronald Edwards turned himself over to the authorities. He had been a fugitive for three years. Again, it was fingerprints that proved to be the undoing of a train robber.

His prints had been found on the paper that had been used to wrap the bank money. This information was presented to the jury at Edward's trial in December.

Ronald Edwards was found guilty.

His sentence: 15 years.

An alert public, careless criminals, and expert detective work had all proved to be the ruin of the great train robbery bandits.

The next robber to be captured was Charles Wilson. He was arrested in Canada, two years after Ronald Edwards had lost his own bid for freedom. In 1968, Wilson was returned to prison to finish his sentence. This was four years after his original conviction and subsequent escape. Police, in following a friend of Wilson, were led to the fugitive.

By this time, Bruce Reynolds, now living in France, was having his own problems. Reynolds was rapidly running out of money. In his desperation, Reynolds took a gamble. He decided to return to England. It was a big mistake. For in no place was he as sought after as in London. And in no other country was he so readily recognizable as in England. But desperate men do desperate things, and can be very careless in the process.

Reynolds seemed to invite capture. Indeed, there were moments when he boasted about who he was. It was only a matter of time before he would be joining the others behind British bars.

That time came in the fall of 1968. After five years of being a fugitive from justice, Bruce Reynolds was captured by police. It was an old story. The main witness against Reynolds at his trial were his own fingerprints. They had been found on items recovered from Leatherslade Farm.

Bruce Reynolds went on trial in January of 1969.

The verdict: Guilty!

The sentence: 25 years!

Now British police and their counterparts around the world could focus their efforts on the last of the great train robbers who still remained a fugitive.

Ronald Arthur Biggs.

In the summer of 1965, Ronald Biggs escaped from prison following the pronouncement of his 30-year sentence. He went to France, and then to Australia. He remained in Australia until 1969, when pictures of Biggs appeared in the Australian media. Despite his plastic surgery, Biggs was in danger of being recognized. Identities of his family were circulated, and it would not be long before they were traced to Biggs.

The wanted train robber fled Australia with the police breathing down his neck. His family remained behind. There was no point in endangering them further. Besides, they would only slow him down, if not inadvertently lead police to him.

From Australia, Biggs went to Central America and, eventually, Brazil. As this book is being written (February, 1979), Ronald Arthur Biggs remains a free man in Brazil.

Yet how can this be if police know where he is?

The answer lies in Brazilian law. The law states that a person who has children born in Brazil cannot be thrown out of the country. As it turned out, a woman who was Biggs' girlfriend told authorities that she was expecting a child and that Biggs was its father. Thus he was beyond the reach of British police.

Biggs is the only one of the great train robbery gang who did not serve a major part of his sentence, which still hangs over his head. As for the others, all eventually were released on parole, except for William Boal, who died in prison in 1970 (the same year that the train driver died, by the way). The last train robber to be freed was Charles Wilson, in June of 1978.

The great train robbery spawned more than a half-dozen books and numerous magazine and newspaper articles. It had also been cited in the 1978 edition of the Guinness Book of World Records as "the greatest recorded train robbery. . . ."

Most of the money has never been recovered. But there is one final irony.

The money stolen from the royal British mail train in the morning hours of August 8, 1963, is no longer legal currency in Britain.

Chapter 3

THE LEGIONNAIRES' DISEASE

For years the killer had eluded scientists. Time after time it struck, silently, invisibly. No one could be sure when and where it would strike next. No one had ever seen it. Fortunately, not all the attacks were fatal. Most of its victims did survive, although they were left, temporarily, disabled. But many did die from the assault upon their bodies.

Year after year, scientists relentlessly, stubbornly, pursued their unknown quarry. Then, one day, they trapped it. For the first time the killer was seen and identified. It was even given a name: *Legionella pneumophila.* But this was the scientists' name for it. Most people would know it by its more common name: *Legionnaires' disease.* And this is its story.

It was the summer of 1968. The place: Pontiac, Michigan. In the course of one week, nearly every single worker at the Oakland Public Health Center became ill with aches, chills, and fever. And no one knew why. A call for help went out to the Center for Disease Control (CDC), in Atlanta, Georgia. The Center for Disease Control is a health arm of the United States government. Its chief concern is controlling the spread of disease, trying to prevent epidemics. The staff is made up of doctors and specialists, as well as laboratory technicians. These are the detectives. And they are engaged in a never-ending struggle against a foe which is invisible to the human eye: the germ, also known as "the bug."

In response to the appeal for aid, the Center for Disease Control dispatched members of its Epidemic Intelligence Service (EIS). It was not long before a trio of investigators arrived on the scene of the attacks that they, also, were struck down. And so another trio was sent. Again, the unknown assailant struck. The mystery deepened. But now the disease, though still unidentified, was given a name. The medical detectives called it "Pontiac Fever." This would be of little consolation to the second group of Epidemic Intelligence Service Investigators. They were taken ill, just like their predecessors.

The health center had become a huge carrier of illness. Strict security measures were taken. No one was allowed to enter the building unless he or she had specific business there, such as the medical detectives. In some ways this was not necessary. The general population avoided it like the plague the building seemed to contain.

Pontiac Fever resembled a flu, but it was not the flu. Symptoms included chills that caused the victim to shake. Yet, at the same time, a victim could be suffering from a burning fever. Other symptoms included exhaustion, muscle pains, and a headache. And some of those who had recovered became ill again upon re-entering the center.

In an effort to track down this strange malady, researchers investigated the center with the proverbial fine-toothed comb. They tested the air and the water. They checked the victims' blood.

Nothing.

They tested animals who had been placed in the building. Some of the animals came down wtih pneumonia and died. When bits of lungs from the dead guinea pigs were injected into the embryos of chickens, the embryos died.

The deaths appeared to be the result of infection from a bacterium. But the scientists could not recover it with any of the usual methods.

The cause and source of the bewildering ailment continued to elude scientists. By the process of elimination, however, they were able to rule out food and drinking water as causes of Pontiac Fever.

Then, one day, an investigator for the Center for Disease Control decided to check once more the air-conditioning system. The investigator himself had only recently recovered from a bout with Pontiac Fever.

Taking an engineer with him who also worked for the Center for Disease Control, the investigator probed one of the air-conditioning units located in the basement of the center. This time their search revealed a formation of dirty water, something which should not have been there. The unit was defective.

It was the water, the investigator later discovered, that was infecting the air filtered through the air conditioning. When guinea pigs breathed air that had come in contact with the water, they developed Pontiac Fever. Unfortunately, scientists were unable to isolate the germ in the water that had caused Pontiac Fever.

Eventually, it was business as usual at the health center, after it had been thoroughly cleaned with disinfectants. Pontiac Fever was placed in the Center for Disease Control's file of unsolved cases. But, not taking any chances, CDC investigators stored for future reference samples of blood taken from the disease's victims.

A total of 144 persons had been stricken with

Pontiac Fever that summer in 1968 (including 95 of 100 health-center workers). Fortunately, no one died from the ailment, and the epidemic seemed to spend itself.

Interestingly enough, few of CDC's unsolved cases have involved fatalities. Between the years 1965 and 1975, of a dozen recorded illnesses, only two illnesses caused deaths. One struck infants only (Sudden Infant Death, in Burlington, Vermont). Five babies died in that outbreak. In the other case, in Washington, D.C., 84 persons came down with severe pneumonia, and 14 died. That epidemic took place at St. Elizabeth's Hospital.

But the worst epidemic lay ahead. Its effects would be felt nationwide. Indeed, cases would be reported around the world. And one of the broadest investigations in medical history would be undertaken. Before it would be over, a key would be found to unlock, not one, but several mysteries.

The time: July, 1976. The place: Philadelphia, Pennsylvania. The setting was the Bellevue Stratford Hotel. The site had been chosen for the 58th annual convention of the American Legion. The mood was an especially festive one. The United States had just celebrated its Bicentennial. It was 200 years since the signing of the Declaration of Independence and thousands of Legionnaires had gathered to celebrate in the "City of Brotherly

Love." They had no way of knowing it, of course, but a killer would be joining them.

The convention was held from July 21 to July 24. Actually, there were two conventions in Philadelphia held by the Pennsylvania branch of the American Legion. The central convention itself was held at the Bellevue Stratford. Meanwhile a related convention was composed of Ladies Auxiliary delegates, their families, and Legionnaires who had no primary role in the main convention at the Bellevue Stratford.

The Bellevue Stratford itself was originally built in 1904 and had undergone subsequent modernization. A large hotel, it contained hundreds of rooms, more than a dozen floors, and had at one time or another been home to important dignitaries from presidents to kings. Accordingly, it was the showcase hotel in Philadelphia.

Disaster struck, shortly after the close of the convention. Over a three-day period (July 25-27), 74 persons became ill. They developed such ailments as headaches and chills. By July 31, 117 Legionnaires had joined the sick list, and the first fatalities were recorded. Six people died.

By August 2 — a little over a week after the end of the convention — the death toll had climbed to 12. Authorities now realized they had an epidemic on their hands. The hospitals began to fill with very sick people. Some had fevers as high as 108 degrees.

The Center for Disease Control, in Atlanta, Georgia, was notified. As with the case of Pontiac Fever, an Epidemic Intelligence Service team was dispatched. Heading the unit was Dr. David Fraser. The group arrived during that hectic first week in August.

Eventually, the EIS team was reinforced and became part of one of the broadest efforts to control the spread of an epidemic. Before long, thousands more persons would aid in the hunt for the unknown killer.

By August 9, the death toll had reached 27.

Clues were sought. Theories were formulated and tested. The medical detectives (as well as police detectives) considered the possibility that the Legionnaires may have been poisoned. But no evidence of poison could be found. Gradually, theories were eliminated. It was not poison. Nor gas. Nor a fungus. Nor a virus.

Scientists established standards of evidence to determine the nature and, ultimately, the cause of the mysterious malady. Two types of evidence were set up and two categories of disease were listed.

The more common ailment was given a name that would indelibly mark it for years to come. It was called "Legionnaires' disease." The other sickness was described as "Broad Street pneumonia," named after the geographic site of the outbreak.

To be listed as Legionnaires' disease, the sickness had to include both clinical and epidemiological traits. To meet the clinical test, a sick person had to have the following symptoms: a minimum temperature of about 102 degrees, evidence of pneumonia (which could be seen by an X-ray of the lungs), and a cough.

This clinical evidence was then checked against epidemiological standards. A sick person fell into the epidemiological category if he or she had attended the July American Legion convention or had entered the Bellevue Stratford around that time.

If the victim had not come in contact with the hotel, but had the clinical symptoms, and had been near the hotel, that person was considered to have Broad Street pneumonia. The reasoning behind this theory was based on an important finding by medical detectives. They discovered, during that first week in August, that almost all the persons who had been stricken with illness had visited the Bellevue Stratford, the location of the main convention.

The broadest possible investigation enabled officials to narrow the focus of their efforts as they began to assemble clues. The clearinghouse for accumulated evidence was the Pennsylvania Department of Health.

Other health officials were also alerted and asked to cooperate in the disease hunt. Hospitals throughout the state of Pennsylvania were requested to report if any of their patients were Legionnaires. Public help was also recruited. People were asked to call a special telephone number if they came across suspected cases of Legionnaires' disease. Furthermore, medical detectives relied upon news accounts to help detect the disease.

The American Legion itself participated in the mass probe. On August 8, as victims 26 and 27 died, Pennsylvania and Legion officials sent a plea for help to 10,000 people. This was the number said to have been at the convention in July. They were asked to report to local Legion halls and fill out a lengthy questionnaire.

The survey was related to the activities of the thousands of people who had attended the convention during the four days between July 21 and July 24. Investigators wanted to know if members of the group had used a hotel air conditioner; if they had come into contact with pigeons around the hotel; if they had used ice in their beverages; and if they had smoked any cigarettes distributed free at the convention, and so on.

The enormous task undertaken by medical detectives cannot be exaggerated. Researchers had to sift through more than 3,600 completed surveys that had been returned to them. Then they had to make a comparison between those delegates who had attended the convention and not gotten sick, and those who had attended and had become ill.

Some patients were asked to return to the hotel and retrace their actions. Medical files of hospitalized patients were examined. Hotel employees, as well as patients, were interviewed. Weather records were checked. The bodies of Legionnaires who had died were examined, and tiny parts were removed for testing.

A mountain of information was gathered and analyzed. Investigators even extended their probe as far back as 1974 to check deaths listed as being caused by flu and pneumonia. Files were checked for admissions and emergency-room treatment in Philadelphia hospitals, beginning with July 1, 1976.

Thus scientists were able to determine the first known case of Legionnaires' disease. And it had nothing to do with the convention itself, but took place just before. Prior to the Legion gathering, a woman had gone to a convention of magicians and later had fallen ill. She survived. This particular convention, however, also was at the Bellevue Stratford. (The first recorded death of a Legionnaire was not until July 27.)

As August, 1976, began to disappear into history, it became clear that the worst was over. The disease had begun to spend itself, and scientists could now assess the damages it had wrought. They estimated that the number of persons meeting both clinical and epidemiological criteria for Legionnaires' disease was 182. Of these patients, 149 had attended the Legion convention. One victim was a hotel employee, and the remaining 32 had no legion affiliation. The number of deaths came to 29, most of them Legionnaires.

It was further noted that 39 persons fell into the category of victims of Broad Street pneumonia. This group registered five fatalities.

But if the epidemic had ended, the investigation had not. The medical detectives intensified their efforts. They still did not know what had caused the disease, how it had been spread, or where it had come from. And they would not rest until they had the answers.

In their work, medical detectives were aided by the most modern medical equipment and techniques. These techniques were not, however, limited to scientific researchers alone. Rather, the medical detectives used reasoning shared by their non-medical counterparts. All were looking for the unknown factor, or "X." And whether that "X" was a germ, an outlaw, or a treasure ship, a key had to be found that would help identify it. Investigators, accordingly, asked questions not very different from those asked by detectives during the Great Train Robbery case.

Had there been similar cases in the past? When? Who had been involved? Where had the outbreaks taken place?

Part of the process involves the method of elimination, making use of trial and error. This means untold hours are spent checking and rechecking data and evidence. It means gathering and analyzing clues, in this case, microscopic clues. It means months, even years, of work. And even then there is no guarantee of success. Sometimes, though, the answer is there but is not recognized.

Meanwhile, in Philadelphia, life was returning to normal. The hotel was declared safe. This, however, could not remove the stigma that had become attached to the Bellevue Stratford. In early November, the hotel went out of business. Very few people wanted to spend the night there. Chalk up another victim of Legionnaires' disease.

The months went by, and medical detectives seemed no closer to finding that elusive "X." Summer had ended and fall had come and gone. With little real progress being made, scientists began to wonder if they would ever solve the mystery of an epidemic in that Bicentennial summer in Philadelphia.

December, 1976. Researchers were on the verge of reporting defeat. Perhaps this was to be another unsolved case in the files of the Center for Disease Control. Perhaps it was to be another Pontiac Fever. Still, just maybe, they had overlooked something. They still had to run their tests, check their theories.

But many scientists were discouraged. The number of personnel trying to crack the Legionnaires case had been greatly reduced. There seemed to be none of the intensity and air of urgency that had been so widespread during the hot, summer months.

Nonetheless, there were medical detectives who were not about to quit. One of those was Dr. David Fraser, who had led a field team (sent by the Center for Disease Control) in Philadelphia when the epidemic had first erupted.

In keeping with Center for Disease Control policy, Dr. Fraser tried to make sure that the researchers in the laboratories of the Center were all told about work still in progress on Legionnaires' disease. One of those researchers was Dr. Charles Shepard. Another was Dr. Joseph McDade.

Dr. Shepard was responsible for that part of the Center that dealt with leprosy and rickettsia which is a type of germ. One of his colleagues was Dr. McDade.

On this particular December day, Dr. Fraser went to see Dr. Shepard. In his hands, Fraser held the latest staff report on Legionnaires' disease. By this time, Shepard's people had run blood tests in the slim hope that somehow the Philadelphia epidemic had been caused by a rickettsia. McDade himself had run such tests, but he could find no organism of that type. McDade had been testing the theory that Legionnaires' disease was caused by rickettsia because those germs produced "Q-fever," a form of pneumonia not unlike that in the epidemic.

He did, however, find items that looked like rickettsia but were much too big to be rickettsia. There were not many of these, and so Dr. McDade thought they might be stray bacteria. Accordingly, he put away the slides that contained the blood samples. For the moment, at least, the hunt for the cause of Legionnaires' disease would have to wait until the end of Christmas; it was then that Dr. McDade received the report produced by the staff of the Center for Disease Control.

December 27, 1976. Dr. McDade leafed through the report. Based on information it contained, Dr. McDade thought again of Q-fever and of the possibility, suggested by laboratory tests, that he might be dealing with a new form of rickettsia. This was especially exciting because the last rickettsia had been discovered nearly half a century before. McDade decided to take another look at the slides of blood samples he had filed. The blood on the slides had been taken from victims of Legionnaires' disease, just as tissues had been.

This time he would be particularly careful in his hunt for alien particles in the blood. In short, he was no longer looking exclusively for the rickettsia with which he was familiar.

Studying slide after slide, McDade pursued his

unknown adversary. And then he saw it. In a strange twist, Dr. McDade found himself staring at the very same type of rickettsia-like "bugs" he had spotted months earlier and had discounted because of their large size and lack of number.

This time, however, there were many of them, which to his trained eye told Dr. McDade that there was an infection, and a major one at that. He reported his findings to Dr. Shepard, who looked at the slide himself.

Now Dr. McDade began to retrace his steps in the investigation by re-examining the notes he had taken of his experiments since the previous August. There would be more tests.

In one test, Dr. McDade injected guinea pigs with tissue taken from the lungs of a victim of Legionnaires' disease. The animals died.

Dr. McDade injected more guinea pigs with a solution containing lung tissue from the previous group. Nothing happened. The guinea pigs remained healthy.

Dr. McDade refused to give up. This meant still more tests, still more work. McDade decided he would inject eggs containing chicken embryos with spleen tissue taken from guinea pigs who had died in an earlier test. It was now December 30. Dr. McDade injected the eggs and went home to wait for the results of his latest experiment.

January 6, 1977. By now Dr. McDade had discovered that most of the chicken embryos had died. Upon examining egg samples, under his microscope, McDade discovered they were identical to those over-sized rickettsia-like organisms he had seen before. He still was not sure, however, that this exciting finding was linked to the cause of Legionnaires' disease.

Dr. McDade now began a series of tests that might prove that what he had found were bacteria and that these bacteria were the cause of Legionnaires' disease.

The necessary proof would come through a test for antibodies, which are used in the body's defense system to combat specific diseases. After these antibodies have fought off the germs, the antibodies remain in the bloodstream. Therefore, doctors can determine if a person has been exposed to a certain disease once they find those particular antibodies — associated with that disease — in a person's blood.

In his test for Legionnaires' disease antibodies, Dr. McDade obtained samples of blood taken from its victims. He then inserted the bacteria he had grown in the egg embryos into the blood samples. A link would show up between the bacteria and the victims' antibodies if those antibodies took the offensive against these germs. Not taking any chances, Dr. McDade, Dr. Shepard, and some of their colleagues tested many blood samples. Nor did they limit their samples just to the blood of Legionnaires. The scientists had to isolate the specific antibody to the newly-found bacteria. And so they tested the bacteria, suspected of causing Legionnaires' disease, with the blood of ordinary pneumonia victims.

Success!

The medical detectives discovered that the bacteria associated with Legionnaires' disease did *not* draw antibodies to it when tested against the blood of standard pneumonia victims. Antibodies, however, *did* attack the bacteria introduced into the blood samples of Legionnaires' disease victims.

Scientists had discovered a new type of bacterium, and it was this new bacterium that was the cause of Legionnaires' disease.

Furthermore, using the same methods, scientists were able to show that, in most cases, what had been called Broad Street pneumonia was really Legionnaires' disease.

If the Legionnaires' bacterium had also caused Broad Street pneumonia, scientists reasoned, was it not also possible that it had been to blame for other diseases, as well? This was what Dr. Charles Shepard had in mind when he decided to run an experiment to check for a link between Legionnaires' disease and an epidemic of pneumonia in 1965. This epidemic had taken place at St. Elizabeth's Hospital, in Washington, D.C., and had killed 14 persons.

It was in this area of research (comparing and analyzing blood and tissue samples) where the Center for Disease Control earned its reputation as the center for U.S. disease control. Over the years, the Center had built up a vast storehouse of blood and tissue samples. Such samples are kept refrigerated to protect them from spoiling, and some have been saved for more than 20 years. The number of individual samples has been listed as over a quarter million!

It was from this huge reservoir of material that Dr. Shepard drew blood samples that had been obtained from victims of the pneumonia epidemic at St. Elizabeth's. That outbreak, by the way, also took place in the summer, in the exact same month — July — as both Legionnaires' disease and Pontiac Fever.

Dr. Shepard had long suspected a possible link between Legionnaires' disease and the pneumonia at St. Elizabeth's because they were similar. Now he was going to try to prove it. Shepard tested blood samples of St. Elizabeth's patients against the Legionnaires' disease bacterium.

They matched!

Another mystery was solved!

Medical detectives now turned their attention to Pontiac Fever. They followed the same testing procedures as before. And again they were successful! The conclusion was beyond doubt: Legionnaires' disease, the pneumonia epidemic at St. Elizabeth's, and Pontiac Fever were all one and the same disease, caused by the same type of bacterium! The researchers decided it was time to go public with the news of their great breakthroughs.

January 18, 1977. The Center for Disease Control announced to the nation that it had discovered a bacterium "quite definitely associated with the disease" that had struck the Legion convention in Philadelphia, in the summer of 1976. The relationship between Legionnaires' disease and the other previous illnesses (Pontiac Fever and St. Elizabeth's pneumonia) was also reported. Credit for the Legionnaires' disease breakthrough was given to Drs. Joseph McDade and Charles Shepard.

Press coverage was widespread and one newspaper ran an editorial titled "The Case of the Baffling Bacterium." But the medical detectives could not rest on past achievements. There was still much work to be done. They still had to determine how the disease had been spread, from where it had come, and how best it could be treated. The latter question turned out to be the easiest one to answer, since researchers now knew what they were looking for. Further tests showed that Legionnaires' disease responded best to a drug called "erythromycin."

Each day's work, and each new test, brought medical detectives closer to solving past mysteries. For example, in April, 1977, at a Center for Disease Control conference, it was reported that Legionnaires' disease had struck persons attending a convention held by the Independent Order of Odd Fellows. The year: 1974. The place: Philadelphia, Pennsylvania. The site of the convention: the Bellevue Stratford.

By now, of course, medical detectives knew that Legionnaires' disease had been around for a long time. They also learned that the "bug" was not limited to the Bellevue Stratford, nor to Pennsylvania. Indeed, cases of Legionnaires' disease have been reported from New York to California.

It was in New York, in fact, where Legionnaires' disease took one of the worst tolls since the Philadelphia epidemic. An outbreak of the illness in New York City, in late summer of 1978, killed 3 people, and sent another 41 to the hospital. Before the year was out, medical detectives had discovered the Legionnaires' disease bacterium in the air-conditioning cooling tower on the rooftop of Macy's department store. Scientists, however, would not blame the tower as the source of the epidemic. The air conditioning unit was disinfected and declared safe.

Legionnaires' disease, however, is not limited to the United States. In April, 1978, the World Health Organization reported that Legionnaires' disease was responsible for the deaths of a number of Europeans, several years *before* the outbreak at the American Legion convention in Philadelphia.

Concern for the scope of the disease, as well as for its effects, was dramatically illustrated when a conference of hundreds of scientists from more than a score of countries was called. By that time, Legionnaires' disease had been reported on several continents.

The most important findings, however, had been made in the case of the Legionnaires' disease. Doctors know what causes the illness, and they know how to treat it. Many lives will be saved that might otherwise have been lost, because of the work of such scientists as McDade, Shepard, Fraser, and many others.

What is especially impressive is that it took only about five months to identify the cause of Legionnaires' disease. By comparison, it took scientists *500 years* to discover the cause of bubonic plague!

In an editorial, *The New England Journal of Medicine* called the discovery of the Legionnaires' disease bacterium "a saga of medical science at its best."

The saga continued. Experts at the Center for Disease Control estimated that Legionnaires' disease strikes as many as 45,000 people each year, killing about 6,000. Yet Legionnaires' disease is thought to be responsible for only a tiny percentage (perhaps 1½ percent) of all reported instances of pneumonia each year in the United States. Looked at another way, this means that the chances are 1.5 in 100 that a person who has pneumonia is suffering from Legionnaires' disease.

Meanwhile, many theories were propounded as to the source of the Legionnaires' disease bacterium, as well as how it was transmitted.

Researchers at the Center for Disease Control, however, seem to have discounted such carriers of the disease as food, insects, water (used for drinking), and person-to-person contact. The latter finding means that Legionnaires' disease is not contagious. Experts at the Center for Disease Control believe that chances are good that the disease is spread through the air. Again, theories must be considered. Dr. David Fraser, of the Center for Disease Control, believes that the Legionnaires' disease bacterium may have many homes.

One major breakthrough took place in the summer of 1978, in Bloomington, Indiana, a site of a Legionnaires' disease outbreak. At Indiana University, a score of persons were stricken. The vast majority had stayed at the Indiana Memorial Union Hotel. Several people died in that outbreak. Medical detectives, upon investigating, discovered the Legionnaires' disease bacterium on a roof unit connected with the air conditioning. They also found the bug in samples of water recovered from a stream running not far from the student building.

Before we leave our story of Legionnaires' disease, there is this last footnote to be related. In November, 1976, the Bellevue Stratford Hotel went out of business, three months after the epidemic had been discovered. People were still worried that if they stayed there, they might become sick. The hotel couldn't even rent rooms to members of out-of-town baseball teams. Finally, it just had to close its doors.

Eventually, the hotel was sold and its possessions were auctioned off. Everything from pianos to carpets, drapes to barber chairs, silverware to dishes were sold to the public. Among the buyers were veterans of the 1976 Legion convention. They were back in Philadelphia for the 60th meeting of their organization.

The new owners of the hotel announced that it was being renovated and would reopen under the name of the Fairmont Hotel. Work began in late 1978. Opening date of the new hotel was 1979.

It is possible that visitors to the new Fairmont may not have to worry about Legionnaires' disease, any more than visitors to any other hotel in the U.S. On November 14, 1978, researchers announced that they had successfully vaccinated laboratory mice and other animals, thus giving them protection against the disease.

Chapter 4

THE CHOWCHILLA KIDNAPPING

The first sign that anything unusual had happened to Ed Ray's school bus came when worried parents began to phone the office of the school superintendent at about 4:30 in the afternoon of July 15, 1976.

Even then there was no cause for immediate worry. There were all sorts of possible mishaps, none of them necessarily serious, that might have happened to the bus. Perhaps it was a flat tire that was delaying it. Or maybe the engine had overheated.

But an hour later, when the bus was still overdue, the police were called, and then the Federal Bureau of Investigation. A search for the missing bus was begun, and at about 8 o'clock that evening it was found, abandoned. A pilot had spotted it from his plane and had led searchers to a waterless creek called Berenda Slough, some five miles to the south and west of Chowchilla, which is located in the heart of California, with a population of 4,600.

Upon investigating, detectives were surprised to find no footprints near the bus. They did, however, find two pairs of tire tracks nearby. It did not take them long to reach a conclusion as to what may have happened to the riders of the bus. The keys to the bus were missing, and the engine had been shut off. Some of the children's belongings had been left behind. There were no signs of violence to indicate an attack. But all these pieces of evidence pointed to one thing.

Kidnapping.

The news of the suspected kidnapping was reported from coast to coast. At the White House, then-President Gerald Ford offered the services of the federal government, in addition to those of the FBI.

In California, Governor Jerry Brown committed the state highway patrol and the national guard to action. A massive hunt was begun for the children, the bus driver, and their abductors. The story, however, was perhaps closest (with the exception of the Chowchilla residents) to parents everywhere whose children were bused to and from school. This particularly applied to those who lived in the more remote sections of the country.

While police scientists checked the bus and surrounding area for additional clues, detectives went door to door in the hope of obtaining information that would be helpful to them. One such report came from a woman who had noticed two vans, one of which — a white van — had been kept in front of her home during the night. She also recalled the date. It was the 14th, the day before the kidnapping. More important, however, this witness had written down the California license plate number of the white van. It was, she noted, 1C91414.

Not all the tips were helpful. Some came from people who were emotionally disturbed. Others were from well-meaning citizens, but the information they had was of no value to police. Still, law enforcement officials could not take chances and had to verify each possible lead.

Many questions remained unanswered. Why had the children been kidnapped? And by whom? Where were these persons now? And the most terrifying question of all could not be answered: Were the children and their bus driver still alive?

Thursday, July 15, 1976. The nightmare begins.

Edward Ray's school bus arrived at the Dairyland Union Elementary School. Summer session was nearly over, and Ed Ray's passengers happily boarded his bus. By 3:50 p.m., the bus, with 31 students aboard, was ready to roll.

The first few stops were uneventful. In the interval, five children got off the bus. The bus now carried 26 children. They ranged in age from five to 14.

The bus was now about a mile away from its next stop. Suddenly, Ed Ray was forced to hit the brakes. A white van was blocking the road. As Ray approached the vehicle, a man with a stocking mask covering his face jumped out.

He had a gun.

The masked figure brandishing the weapon ordered Ray to open the school bus door. He then told the bus driver to move to the rear of the bus, and ordered the children to do the same.

Two more masked figures joined the unfolding drama. One replaced Ray in the driver's seat. One remained with the white van. Once more, the bus began to move followed by the white van that had originally forced it to stop.

After a while, the bus came to a halt, and Ray noticed a green van alongside of the road. Ray and the 19 girls and seven boys were ordered to leave the bus. They were divided into two groups. One group was herded into the green van. The other, into the white van. Ray tried to remember one of the license plates. But all he could memorize were the numbers "414."

The vans were sealed, and began to move.

No one could be sure how long they had been riding. And an atmosphere of terror was mingled with inadequate ventilation, virtually no light, no food or water, and no sanitary facilities. These hardships served to make the journey seem longer. Some of the children became ill.

The vans finally stopped moving. A long, painful, terrifying hour passed before anything followed. Then a voice came out of the darkness ordering Ray to leave the bus first, to be followed by the children.

They stumbled out of the vans into further darkness. The two vans had parked with their rear doors facing a pit, several feet across. The pit was covered in such a way that the captors could see nothing else but the underground opening and the vans.

Ray was asked his name and age. He was told to remove his pants and boots. After the bus driver had complied, the masked figures gave him a flashlight and a couple of additional batteries. They were going to be buried alive, and there was nothing they could do about it.

Desperately, Ed Ray pleaded with the kidnappers. He told them that he wanted to see his grandchildren again. His plea was ignored. One of the children spoke up, trying to find out what the kidnappers wanted from them. She was told to remain silent.

Ray climbed down a ladder into a pit. The bus driver found himself inside of what appeared to be another van. It had been outfitted with mattresses and box springs. Old bedspreads and drapes substituted for blankets.

For food, the kidnappers had left a jar of peanut butter, two loaves of bread, two bags of potato chips, a box of dry cereal, and 10 plastic jugs each containing five gallons of water. Two holes, at the bottom of their prison, were to be used as toilets by the captives. Finally, to provide air, the kidnappers had installed a system of air hoses and fans. The system was run by batteries. It was only a matter of time before the batteries would be dead, and the captives, too.

At the bottom of the pit, Ed Ray looked at his watch. The time was 3:30 in the morning. It was now Friday; Ray and the children had been gone for 11 hours.

One at a time, the rest of the children were ordered into the pit to join their bus driver. Like him, they were asked their names, and told to surrender some of their clothing. Some of the children were also ordered to give the kidnappers personal articles they had had on them when they had left school. These included such items as pencils, string, and small change.

Soon all 26 children had joined Ed Ray in their makeshift, below-the-ground, jail. As the last child entered the pit, the kidnappers withdrew the ladder and flung down a roll of toilet paper to the trapped group.

The top of the pit was closed.

The 27 kidnap victims were now alone. They had been left to the heat, their own filth, the darkness, and a supply of food that would last them only one hour. They were also left with their fears.

Eventually, the fear, the hunger, the exhaustion, and the pain gave way to sleep. While the children slept, Ed Ray thought of escape. He believed that the kidnappers were going to let the children, and him die. Ray glanced at his watch. It was 4 p.m. They had now been buried alive for 13 hours. And they had been missing for some 24 hours.

The bus driver told the children that they were going to escape. Working with some of the older boys, Ray began a pile of mattresses and box springs, one on top of the other, in a corner of the van. It was their hope to reach the opening in the roof, through which they had originally entered.

Soon the other children joined the escape efforts. The tower of bedding was completed. Ray climbed to the top and tried to shove open the ceiling lid. It wouldn't move. The bus driver then spied a short, thick, wooden board. With this new tool, Ray was able to move the lid a little, by placing the board betwen the lid and the ceiling. This took some doing because the lid was made of iron, and nearly a half inch in thickness.

The metal lid began to yield more and more, grudgingly. Ray could now see that two huge batteries, each weighing many pounds, had been placed over the metal lid. By moving the lid further, Ray was able to tilt the batteries toward him and let them rest against the mattresses. The batteries were then removed to the rear of the van.

Ray could now move the sheet more easily. But he was not free yet. The metal had been covered with a box made of plywood. And on top of the box, dirt had been piled.

But Ray could now climb out of the van and on to its roof. He could not, however, stand up because he still had the plywood ceiling to contend with. The 190-pound bus driver then tried to lift the plywood lid, bracing his back against it. It hardly budged.

Ray was taking a big risk, and he knew it. He had no way of knowing how much dirt lay above them. It was possible that he was risking a cave in, and his efforts could bury them all. But it was a chance he had to take.

Using techniques similar to those he had used in squeezing past the metal shield, and again with the aid of the children, Ray was able to move enough of the wood so that they could see natural light. All this took hours of painful, back-breaking work.

Using the makeshift tools they had, stretching muscles to their limits, and clawing away at the dirt, Ray and the children slowly dug their way to freedom. Eventually, they formed a human chain to the outside world and safety. Bus driver Edward Ray was the last one to leave their dungeon. They had been trapped for approximately 16 hours, buried beneath several feet of dirt.

Ray, with his charges in tow, found himself by a construction site, by a large rock quarry. They approached a man who was still at work. When they told him their incredible story, the startled worker said that he had heard reports of the missing school bus broadcast over the radio.

The construction worker also told them that they were in the city of Livermore, about 100 miles to the north and west of Chowchilla.

Within minutes, the police had been summoned and had arrived. The children were given medical care, clean clothes, and food. They were also questioned by law enforcement officials.

By 4 a.m. Saturday, July 17 — some 36 hours after their kidnapping — Edward Ray and the 26 children had returned to Chowchilla. Hundreds of people had gathered to greet the homecomers. Among the throng of well wishers, and concerned parents, were members of the media from across the United States. The Chowchilla kidnapping was big news.

The ordeal of Ed Ray and the children, as well as their friends and families, had ended at last, but their memories had been marked permanently from those terrible hours in captivity. And the case of the Chowchilla school bus hijacking and kidnapping was far from over. With the bus passengers safely in their families' arms once more, the time had come to see that justice was served.

But where should police begin? What clues, if any, did they have?

Essentially, law officers had two vital pieces of evidence. First, and foremost, they had the underground van itself, in which Ray and the children had been imprisoned.

Second, they had a report of a vehicle with license plate number 1C91414. According to the California Department of Motor Vehicles, the vehicle bearing that license plate was a newly registered white van. The date of registration was July 14, the day before the kidnapping. Remaining information about the registration, however, turned out to have been falsified. Still, the DMV was able to help police by providing the identity of the van's previous owner, which turned out to be an agency of the U.S. government, located in California. The agency was connected with the military and disposed of surplus supplies.

Upon further investigation, police found that three vans had been sold by the agency in Alameda. The vans had no side windows since the Navy had used them to move prisoners. The purchaser of the vans, according to government documents, was a person going under the name of "Mark Hall."

At about this time, police had bus driver Ed

Ray placed under hypnosis. They hoped that he would be able to give them more information, including the rest of the license plate of one of the vans. As a result of the hypnosis, Ray was able to recall the full number. It was 1C71414. This did not match the 1C91414 originally reported to police, but the doctor who had hypnotized the bus driver told police that Ray could easily have gotten confused as a result of his ordeal. The doctor was convinced that Ray really meant 1C91414.

Another break for law officers came in the early morning hours of Sunday, July 18, three days after the kidnapping. Hikers came across a suitcase and some clothing that had been thrown down an embankment. The articles were turned over to police. When the police examined the items they discovered a driver's license and picture of Ed Ray. They later found that the clothing had belonged to the children from the bus.

By early Monday, July 19, law officers had identified the moving van (which had been the bus passengers' prison) as belonging to a moving and storage company. When they checked with the company, police were told that the van had been sold in late 1975.

An official of the firm told police that the purchaser had been a young man by the name of Frederick Newhall Woods. As it turned out, Woods was the son of the man who owned the quarry where the buried van had been found.

Police then checked to see if young Woods had a criminal record.

He did.

According to records on file young Woods had been arrested in late 1974. He had originally been charged with auto theft. The charge was reduced, however, and Woods pleaded guilty to tampering. He was fined $125 and placed on probation for one year. He was 22 years old at the time of his arrest.

The records turned out to be more of a gold mine of information than police might have suspected. For along with Woods, two other young men had been arrested and had pleaded guilty to lesser charges regarding the car.

The co-defendants with Woods were two brothers: James Leonard Schoenfeld, 22, and Richard Allen Schoenfeld, 20.

At about this time, law officials received a phone call from an attorney in San Francisco. The attorney told agents of the Federal Bureau of Investigation that he had been called by a man who had identified himself as Dr. John Schoenfeld. This took place on the morning of Saturday, July 17, two days after the kidnapping.

The attorney said the caller had wanted to know if he might agree to defend persons who might be suspected of having taken part in the Chowchilla kidnapping. The lawyer added that the caller further asked if the suspects would be well advised to turn themselves over to police.

He also wanted to know if the suspects, if convicted, might be executed. The attorney told FBI agents he had refused to become involved with the case.

As it turned out, the parents of Richard and James Schoenfeld were Dr. and Mrs. John Schoenfeld. When FBI agents questioned Dr. Schoenfeld, he told them that the call had been made in behalf of one of his patients. He added that he could not tell them the patient's name because he was not allowed to do so under the tradition of doctor-patient confidentiality.

In any event, by Tuesday, July 20 — less than one week after the kidnapping — law officers considered young Fred Woods, and Richard and James Schoenfeld, as the main suspects in the Chowchilla kidnapping case. Under U.S. law, however, the three young men were still innocent. It was up to law enforcement officials to prove the trio's guilt, beyond a reasonable doubt.

In an effort to do so, police checked with the company that provided security for the owners of the quarry and nearby property, where the moving van had been buried, along with the school bus passengers, and their driver.

Police subsequently learned that a person identifying himself as Fred Newhall Woods had been found rummaging through discarded metal at the quarry. Police were also told that the time young Woods had been seen was in December, 1975. By questioning security guards further, as well as checking the records kept by guards based on their rounds, police were able to place young Woods, and possibly Richard Schoenfeld, at the quarry some time before the kidnapping.

A web of evidence was gradually being tightened around young Woods and the two Schoenfeld brothers. Samples of young Woods' handwriting (taken at the time of the 1974 arrest) were matched against a signature on registration documents for a van purchased by "Mark Hall." The papers had been obtained from the California Department of Motor Vehicles. Based on a comparison test, police felt that "Mark Hall" and Fred Woods were one and the same person. The van in question had been the white van bearing the license plate number 1C91414. In similar fashion, police determined that another van had been bought by James Schoenfeld.

Wednesday night, July 21. Less than a week after the kidnapping, police had obtained permission to search the home of young Fred Woods. They were met at the door by his father, who agreed to cooperate with the law officers. Young Woods, however, was not there. His father told police that the family had not seen their son since the day after the kidnapping had taken place, July 16, Friday.

Police next directed their attention to a nearby house on the Woods' property. Detectives had been told that young Woods lived in a part of the house, above the garage. A search of young Woods' living quarters turned up an outline that described how the kidnapping was to be carried out. Police also recovered a ransom note. They now had enough evidence to take young Fred Woods into custody, assuming they could find him.

Detectives later learned that fingerprint experts had found James Schoenfeld's prints on the kidnapping plan. Furthermore, police scientists revealed, the handwriting on the plan and ransom note matched that of James Schoenfeld. The fingerprints of his brother, Richard, were identified on other evidence police had recovered.

Acting on information they had received, law enforcement officials investigated a section of a warehouse that had been rented to one of the suspects, young Fred Woods. Obtaining a search warrant, they entered the premises. Inside they found three vans. One was white. Another was green. The investigators checked the license plate on the white van.

1C91414.

It was the van that bus driver Ed Ray had identified as being used during the kidnapping.

In addition to the vans, police found food, mattresses, a shotgun, and what looked to them to be children's clothing. The web of evidence tightened still further. And for at least one suspect, that pressure seemed too painful to withstand any longer.

On Friday, July 23, eight days after the Chowchilla kidnapping, Richard Schoenfeld surrendered to police.

The night young Schoenfeld turned himself in, police obtained a search warrant and entered the Schoenfeld home. In James Schoenfeld's bedroom, police found the geographic equivalent of Woods' master plan for the bus hijacking and the abduction of the children who rode the school vehicle.

In the room, police found maps. On these maps were marks emphasizing the locations of a number of country schools. One of those checked off was the Dairyland School. Also marked were the places where the bus had been stopped and later hidden.

Police also searched Richard Schoenfeld's room. In there they found authorization for three vans police had seen in the warehouse young Woods had rented.

Law enforcement officers now had the evidence they needed to press charges against the suspected kidnappers.

On Friday, July 23rd, a judge issued arrest warrants for Frederick Newhall Woods, James Leonard Schoenfeld, and Richard Allen Schoenfeld. All were charged with kidnapping and armed robbery. Woods and James Schoenfeld were also charged with being fugitives from justice. Richard was already in jail.

A little more than one week after the kidnapping, police had identified three suspects and charged them with having taken part in the crime. They also had one of the suspects in custody.

Where were the others?

Following the kidnapping, young Fred Woods and James Schoenfeld went to Reno, Nevada. The daring escape of the children and their bus driver destroyed any hope that the kidnappers may have had about collecting a ransom. In fact, they didn't even have time to deliver a demand for money in exchange for the lives of the 27.

Woods and Schoenfeld decided that the wisest thing to do now was to head for Canada. They agreed on a plan. Fred would fly, and James would drive. Their meeting point was the central post office in Vancouver, British Columbia, in western Canada. A schedule was set for them to make their rendezvous. If, after a month, they still had not made contact, then it would be each man for himself.

Accordingly, they went their separate ways. And, on July 17th, Saturday — around dinner time — a man going under the name of Ralph Lester Snider landed at an airport in Vancouver, Canada, That man, in reality, was Frederick Newhall Woods. He had no trouble getting into the country. Nor did he have any trouble renting a room.

Less fortunate was James Leonard Schoenfeld.

Twice, young Schoenfeld tried to enter Canada. And twice he was turned away by border officials. The first time, under Canadian questioning, Schoenfeld admitted to having a criminal record. On Schoenfeld's second attempt, Canadian officials searched his car and found weapons. Schoenfeld was taken into custody. Police, however, decided to let him go after they had called their American counterparts and were told that neither the guns nor the car were being sought by police. Arrest warrants still remained to be issued for either Schoenfeld, his brother, or Woods.

James Schoenfeld returned to the United States.

On Sunday, July 24th, he was back in California. By now, both he and young Fred Woods had read the news that Richard Schoenfeld had surrendered to police. Both were now also hunted men.

James decided that the time had come for him to follow his brother and give himself up, on Thursday, July 29th.

He never got the chance.

Since police were not told that young Schoenfeld was going to surrender to them, they still considered him a fugitive and were combing the countryside for him. While calling his father from a public phone, Schoenfeld had been seen. The witness reported this sighting to the Federal Bureau of Investigation, along with the license plates of the vehicle Schoenfeld had been driving.

Thursday, July 29th.

Young Schoenfeld was driving on a California highway when another motorist recognized the car and driver from news reports and published photographs of the fugitives. The motorist pulled off the highway and notified police. It did not take them long to give chase.

Schoenfeld was captured.

Two down, one to go.

In custody, James Schoenfeld told police that Fred Woods was in Vancouver. At noon the same day, Canadian police arrested young Fred Woods when he went to the post office to meet James Schoenfeld. They turned him over to the Federal Bureau of Investigation.

On August 26th, Frederick Newhall Woods, James Leonard Schoenfeld, and Richard Allen Schoenfeld were officially charged with kidnapping and armed robbery. The charges also included physically harming their victims. If convicted, they could be sentenced to life in prison, with no chance of parole.

They pleaded not guilty.

All legal efforts on behalf of the trio were exhausted after a struggle that would last more than a year.

In late July, 1977, Fred Woods, James Schoenfeld, and Richard Schoenfeld pleaded guilty to kidnapping. The charges of armed robbery that had been placed against them were dropped. The three young men were now fighting to avoid spending the rest of their lives in prison. If convicted of harming any of the children during the kidnapping, the three — all in their early 20s — would be sentenced to remain in jail until they died.

In a separate trial, they would face some of the children and the bus driver whom the three had kidnapped the year before, and whom they had buried alive.

The trial lasted until mid-December. The defendants had voluntarily given up their right to a jury trial. It did not take the presiding judge long to deliver his verdict.

Guilty!

Under California law, the judge had no alternative in passing sentence in a case of kidnapping where bodily harm had been proved beyond a reasonable doubt.

On February 17, 1978, James Leonard Schoenfeld and Frederick Newhall Woods were sentenced to life in prison, without possibility of parole. At the time of sentencing, both men were 26 years old.

The only one who had a chance for eventual freedom was Richard Allen Schoenfeld. He, too, had been sentenced to spend the rest of his life in prison. Because of his age, however (23 at the time of sentencing, but 22 at the time of his arrest), California law stipulated that Richard Schoenfeld might some day be released on parole.

As a footnote, it should be mentioned that in 1976 the Associated Press proclaimed the Chowchilla bus hijacking and kidnapping as the most important story of the year.

For the people of Chowchilla — especially for those who were participants in the drama of the kidnapping — it is a story that will long be remembered.

Chapter 5

THE SEARCH FOR "ROOTS"

Alex Haley had never wanted to be a writer. If he had, he might have taken notes when he was a boy growing up in Henning, Tennessee, about 50 miles north of Memphis.

As it was, he would sit quietly on his grandmother's porch, on those soft, summer evenings when a number of relatives would gather and tell — as they so often did — the history of their family, in the United States.

Invariably, their story would begin with someone called "the African," who called himself "Kinte." They told how this African had been captured by slave traders while he had been searching for wood to cut for a drum, and of his subsequent voyage to America. The time was in the middle to late 1700s.

Kinte, the story went, landed at (what Haley's relatives called) "Napolis." He was then sold into slavery to work at the plantation of a "Massa John Waller," in Spotsylvania County, Virginia. But this African was a proud man and refused to be anyone's slave. He tried running away several times, but was caught, brought back, and severely punished. The last time he broke for freedom and was captured, slave catchers cut off part of his foot.

A doctor saved the African's life. This doctor also was the brother of the African's master, and his name was William Waller. William Waller bought Kinte and made him a gardener, because the crippled slave could do no heavy work. The African could no longer hope to escape because of his disability. It was something he would have to learn to live with, just as he would have to learn to be called by the name his owner had given him. He was called "Toby," even though his African first name was Kunta.

Although it was cruel and painful, the loss of a part of Kunta Kinte's foot was in a sense a blessing in disguise. For it limited his ability to do heavy work, and thus greatly reduced his value as a slave. This meant that he could remain on one plantation for many years. This would also enable him to raise and maintain a family, which was unusual for slaves because slave families were often wrenched apart and sold separately by their owners. With parents being sold away from their children, and children from parents, slaves had little opportunity to forge family ties, or keep a family history.

So Kunta Kinte made the most of this opportunity when he married another slave on the plantation. Her name was Bell. Bell and Kunta had a daughter, Kizzy. When Kizzy was old enough to understand, her father told her of his life in Africa until he was kidnapped and sold into slavery. He also taught her words in his native African tongue.

For example, he said a guitar was "ko." A river, "Kamby Bolongo." And his real name, he told Kizzy, was not "Toby," but "Kinte."

Kunta impressed upon Kizzy the importance of knowing her heritage and of passing it on to her children and to their children. After she was sold away from her parents, Kizzy continued this tradition with her own child, a boy, George (known as "Chicken" George for his work with fighting roosters).

And Chicken George continued this tradition after he married Matilda. He told the story of the African to each of his own eight children. George's storytelling, in turn, was picked up by his fourth child, Tom, after Tom married Irene, and they had eight children of their own. The youngest of the Tom Murray children was Cynthia, Alex Haley's maternal grandmother. Haley's great-aunt Liz was Cynthia's sister. (Murray was the name of Tom's master, a plantation owner from Alamance County, North Carolina.)

These stories remained with Alex Haley as he grew up in his grandmother Cynthia's home in Henning, Tennessee, where the family had settled following the Civil War, and the freeing of the slaves.

At the age of 17, Alex Haley enlisted in the Coast Guard. It was during 20 years in service that Haley decided to become a writer. He struggled for many years before he finally became successful, writing books and articles for magazines.

One day, in the early 1960s, Haley found himself in Washington, DC. He had been assigned to do an interview for a magazine. The interview, however, was not scheduled until the afternoon and, it still being morning, Haley was looking for something to do. Realizing that he had never been to the National Archives and was now quite near, Haley decided to go into that building.

While at the Archives, Haley asked to examine the census file for Alamance County, North Carolina, for 1870.

Haley had remembered his grandmother's stories after all.

The 1870 census was the first census to take place after the Civil War, and the first in which blacks were counted by name. Before this, slaves were listed with an "x," with some descriptive material following (such as age and sex), but with no names. A census reader could tell how many slaves an owner had by the number of "x's" near his name.

For about an hour or so, Haley went through the 1870 census. Soon, however, he became bored and decided to leave. On his way out, he went through the room where genealogical records are kept. In this room, Haley saw people engrossed in documents before them. Haley found this deeply moving because he realized that before his eyes were people researching their roots, trying to probe their own identities.

Having experienced this revelation, Haley returned to the room where he had been studying the census for Alamance County, North Carolina, for 1870. The material had remained where he had left it.

Haley spent the next hour studying the information in front of him. Then a name caught his eye. The name was "Tom Murray," a blacksmith. Below that name was written "Irene." Following this, Haley read the names of their children. He recalled the names his grandmother had told him way back when he was growing up in her home in Henning, Tennessee. Then he came across the information "Elizabeth, age 6," and realized that that was his Aunt Liz! (His grandmother had not been born yet.)

The information came as a shock to Haley. Not

because he had not heard all this before from his grandmother, but because what she told him was now confirmed in records held by the United States government!

Unfortunately, all the women who had gathered on his grandmother's porch during those summer days in Henning, Tennessee, were dead. All except for "Cousin Georgia," who was 20 years younger than his grandmother.

Excited, Haley flew to see the elderly woman. When he arrived he related his great discovery to her, and she in turn repeated the family saga he had heard so many times before. Haley told her that he was determined to trace their family origins back to Kunta Kinte. To do so, he would have to find Kinte's homeland.

It was as if Haley was carrying a torch for the family, a torch that would light knowledge of who they really were. He was now determined to learn more about his heritage. To do so, he had to find the source of the African words Kunta Kinte had taught his daughter, Kizzy, centuries before.

In an effort to accomplish this, Haley went to the United Nations, in New York City. He tried time and again to get information from African diplomats. But he was unsuccessful. No one could understand the words Haley spoke, at least not the way he pronounced them.

Haley then turned for help to a long-time friend, a man who was an expert at conducting research. The friend gave Haley a list of names of experts in African languages. Haley turned out to be especially interested in an individual who taught at the University of Wisconsin. This Midwestern professor had lived in Africa and had written a book on oral history.

The professor agreed to do what he could to help Haley. He also consulted other experts who might be able to provide Haley with clues to the birthplace of Kunta Kinte, "the African."

Based on the information Haley gave them, and their own intimate knowledge of Africana, the experts told Haley that the words he had heard from his grandmother probably were from the "Mandinka" tongue, spoken by the "Mandingo" people.

For example, they told Haley that the word "ko," probably referred to "ko-ra," a musical instrument played by the Mandingo. And "bolongo," meant "river." So, "Kamby Bolongo," the experts said, may refer to "Gambia River." Accordingly, Haley decided that he must visit the country of The Gambia, in West Africa.

But to Haley, Africa in general, and The Gambia in particular, were subjects he knew virtually nothing about. He did know that one did not just run off willy-nilly to Africa. He needed help.

But who?

Haley's best bet, he knew, was to seek out someone from The Gambia itself, but who was now living in the United States. Someone who might be willing to return to Africa with Haley to help the journalist find his ancestral homeland.

In Washington, D.C., Haley went to the U.S. State Department. He was told that there were many African students in the United States. In fact, Haley was told, there were literally thousands! There were, however, only a dozen from The Gambia. The student closest to Haley attended a college in New York State. Haley was given the name of the college and the student.

The student agreed to help, and the two men flew to The Gambia.

Once in Africa, Haley was introduced to the student's father. The father, in turn, introduced the author to several men who were familiar with their country's history and tradition. The men told Haley of still other men, known as "griots," who were the historians of African villages. For the villages in which they lived, these griots kept the village's history memorized. They were living history books, capable of relating information that covered hundreds of years.

These men also produced a map for Haley to look at. Then they told him that villages that were extremely old were given the names of the people who had put down their roots there. Such was the case of "Kinte." The men told Haley that "Kinte" was a famous name in The Gambia, and that it went back many years in its history.

In agreeing to do what they could for Haley, the men said they would try to locate the griot who was familiar with Kinte history. On this note of hope, Haley returned to America.

Haley left Africa with these promises of further assistance from the people he met, it was true. But he also realized how much work he would have to do on his own. He had very little knowledge of things African.

Haley then embarked on a period of intensive research, reading as much as he could on the subjects of West Africa, and slavery. In addition to his own readings, Haley was given information by volunteers eager to help. Some of that information came from material they had read, such as Harold Courlander's book, *The African*.

And then one day it came.

A letter from Africa.

But Haley had no money left for such an expensive trip.

Seeking funding, Haley contacted people whom he knew from his work for *The Reader's Digest*. They agreed to help.

Encouraged, and with money to support his efforts, Haley now returned to Africa, heeding the request of the letter he had received, asking him to do so.

A griot had been found.

Would he be able to tell the story of Kunta Kinte?

* * *

When Haley had arrived in The Gambia, there was no griot waiting to meet him. The only way Haley was going to meet him was to visit the old man, upriver. This meant Haley would have to organize a safari.

And so he did. On this safari, Haley included, as he had been instructed, interpreters and musicians. The latter were to entertain the griot as he recited the story of Kunte Kinte.

Soon the day came. Haley and his entourage arrived in the village of Juffure, in The Gambia. There they met the griot who, in Mandinka, began to relate his knowledge of the family Kinte.

The old man spoke for many hours, starting from the beginning, in the distant past. He talked about who married whom, and the names of their children. He also recalled important events.

Then he mentioned that during the years 1750 to 1760, Kunta Kinte was born. He had been the first of the four sons of Omoro Kinte and Binte Kebba.

Then the griot said that "about the time the king's soldiers came," Kunta Kinte had left his village to chop wood to make a drum. He was never seen again.

Haley was stunned! He was hearing his grandmother's words all over again, from the lips of this stranger thousands of miles from Henning, Tennessee!

Alex Haley had found his roots at last!

There was much excitement and tears of joy

throughout the village as Haley told the griot that the author had heard the same tale from his grandmother and his Cousin Georgia, who had died while Haley was in Africa.

When Haley finally left Juffure, The Gambia, and Africa, and flew home to the United States, he had made up his mind that he was going to write a book. And he was going to call that book, *Roots*. It would take 12 years of his life, nine to research, and three to write.

But he had to know more.

Based on the information his grandmother and the griot had given him, and on his own readings, Haley knew that Kunta Kinte had been kidnapped from The Gambia, via the Gambia River. He had been brought across the ocean to the port of Annapolis, Maryland, what Haley's grandmother had called "Napolis."

But Haley did not know the name of the slave ship, at this point, nor the date when Kunte Kinte was kidnapped. All the griot had told him was that Kunta had been captured "about the time the king's soldiers came."

This clue brought Haley to London, England. Checking British records, Haley discovered that British soldiers had been ordered to defend an English slave fort on the Gambia River. The year was 1767 when these troops had been dispatched from England to Africa.

Haley next studied maritime records of slave ships. Using these records, at the Public Records

Office, Haley traced a slave ship destined for Annapolis, Maryland. Following up this lead, he returned to the United States.

Haley's quest took him to the Library of Congress, in Washington, DC, and the Maryland Hall of Records, in Baltimore. With the aid of archivists and other specialists, Haley was able to determine that the name of the slave ship was the *Lord Ligonier*. It had been built in New Hampshire in 1765, and its first voyage had taken it from Maryland to England. From England, the ship went to Africa to the land of The Gambia to pick up cargo, including slaves, and then returned to Maryland.

All this work took many weeks of going through files of slave ships that had gone from England to Africa, and then to Colonial America.

Continuing his search, Haley examined local newspapers published around the time the *Lord Ligonier* had gone through Annapolis customs: September 29, 1767. In one such newspaper, Haley came across an advertisement for slaves to be sold.

Based on the information given to him by his grandmother, Haley had then gone to Richmond, Virginia, to study legal deeds for Spotsylvania County. The information inspiring Haley was that Kunta Kinte had been sold to John Waller in Spotsylvania, and then to Waller's brother, William. Haley also knew that Kunta Kinte's master had named the slave, "Toby."

Haley checked the records after the time the *Lord Ligonier* landed in Annapolis. In a deed dated September 5, 1768, Haley found that William Waller had obtained a slave from John Waller. The deed said that John Waller had given William Waller property. And this property included "a man slave named Toby."

Toby, whose name was really Kunta Kinte, was Alex Haley's great-great-great-great grandfather, and the forebear of seven generations.

Epilogue:

There had been nothing like it in the history of television. If any American phoned a friend or relative at home on the evenings of January 23 to January 30, 1977, chances are that person was watching *Roots.*

Roots was a mini-series, 12 hours in length, that chronicled the story of journalist Alex Haley's ancestors. Based on his best-selling book, *Roots: The Saga of An American Family*, the 8-part series documented the legacy left by Kunta Kinte.

It has been said that more people watched *Roots*, especially the concluding chapter, than any other program in television history. During those January days, nine out of every 10 homes in the United States with television sets were tuned to *Roots*. This translated into 130 million viewers, at one time or another, with 80 million following *Roots* on the last night it was presented.

A little over two years later, *Roots II: The Next Generations* continued the saga, bringing the story up to modern times, including Haley's search for Kunta Kinte — and the journalist's encounter with the griot.

Again, tens of millions of Americans tuned in. What they ultimately saw was one man who had reclaimed a lost heritage. And in so doing, he had answered his own question, concerning who he was.

He now knew from where he had come.